The Actor's Edge

THIS BOOK IS DESIGNED to give beginners an "edge" in the increasingly competitive profession of acting and to help fore-stall the frustration that comes from lack of well-directed, highly disciplined preparation!

With motion pictures, television, and commercials, made for TV movies, and numerous other film/video projects, talent is being burned up at an incredible pace! There will always be an open door for the professional, well-trained, highly disciplined actor, whether just starting out or a well-seasoned pro.

After twenty-five years experience, an actor/drama coach presents the fundamental theories of acting and their practical applications. Mr. Pennington sets forth the basic techniques. Actors receive the result of years of Mr. Pennington's own studies, from participation in the motion picture business as an actor and well-known teacher and from experience gained during many successful years of guiding beginners and professionals in the fundamentals and advanced techniques of acting—learning how to talk, sit, stand, breathe and speak effectively, when to move, when to pause, how to analyze a role and how to develop a characterization. The advanced techniques of acting and public speaking are thoroughly covered and will be of equal value to the public speaker and politician, as well as the beginning actor. In addition it will be useful to professionals, who have already launched careers and teachers who want to review, consolidate and amplify their knowledge for the advancement of their careers.

THE ACTOR'S EDGE

by Renowned
Dramatic Coach

—Lee Pennington

Marble Falls Press
P. O. Box 1727
Marble Falls, Texas 78654

Library of Congress Catalog in Publication Number
95-81869

ISBN Number 0-9650309-0-3

Cover Illustration by Dale Wilkins

Printed in the United States of America
at Morgan Printing in Austin, Texas

This book is dedicated
to my dear wife,
Janet,
and our sons,
Justin & Jon

Acknowledgements

My grateful appreciation goes to those people whose loyalty, confidence and support fired the drive for a multifaceted career as an actor and teacher.

I especially want to recognize Tom Drake, James Best, Isabelle Draesmer, Spring Byington, Ruth Burch, Earl Felton, Dack Rambo, Tammy Lynn, Dee Mancini, James Brolin, Elvis Presley, Bill Bixby, Earl Barton, Tim Wade and my buddy, Russ Larson

and in memory of

Milton S. Davis

whose inspiration saw me through Boot Camp, and the open doors of Hollywood. I would also like to give a big thank you to Mary Ann Fletcher for her thorough and complete editing job, plus the time she gave so unselfishly for the betterment of this book.

Table of Contents

A Star is the one
who develops these best

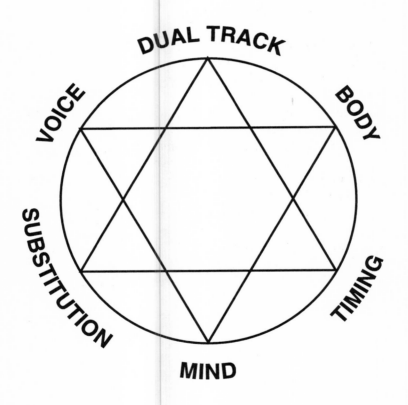

DUAL TRACK

VOICE

BODY

SUBSTITUTION

TIMING

MIND

Introduction

After twenty-five years of making a living as an actor and drama coach, studying with the great teachers and learning on my own, this book is presented with all of my experience, strength, hope, and heart.

With hopes the information herein will not be lost or forgotten, but passed on to another generation, I humbly attempt to set forth the truth about the keys that unlock the many doors to acting.

There are sadly few left that *know* the truth, that were taught the basic laws and principles upon which to build a career in the acting field. Much of the information herein has been unavailable up until now! As years have passed since the days of "Studio Stars," where raw material was made into stars, where a $50.00 a week clerk could become a significant personality in the star system of large studios. They made their own stars, taught them, groomed, nurtured, and publicized them; in short, they built almost every facet of their life to fit the mold. I'm talking about such stars as Clark Gable, Shirley Temple, Lucille Ball, Gary Cooper, Ronald Regan, Betty Grable, and Cary Grant to name just a few.

All of the same things they were taught is what this book is all about. But this book is about *acting*, not actors or personalities; therefore, the limited use of famous names.

CHAPTER ONE

The Emotional Physician
(And His Tradition)

In your desire to be a serious actor, you are applying for membership in the oldest brotherhood of emotional physicianship known to mankind. The duty of the actor is great. Thousands of years before the birth of Christ, acting served the same purpose that it is serving today.

Fundamentally it has not changed from the time cave men formed circles in ritualistic and pantomimic dances, thus stirring emotional responses from their audiences.

All through the ages the challenge of the actor has been to inspire. As the human race progressed, instinct gave way to inspiration. Inspiration became a creative tool of civilization. To be aware of creation born of inspiration and to be able to direct that creation is a direct result of intelligence.

It has always been the function of the actor to be the *emotional physician*, who gives solace and encouragement to those who need it—when they need it.

As civilization was propelled onward, the worth of the actor became obvious. Physical and spiritual service, plus emotional ease, rest and stimulus, all emanate from the actor to the audience.

The actor must be a fine individual. He must truly possess the fruit of the spirit and approach his calling with authority, humility, and fearlessness. He is a torch bearer and a fearless trail-blazer into an expanding frontier.

The actor should be full of enthusiasm for every phase of life. The more he becomes aware of, the more he increases his stature as an individualist. The exact qualities he possesses are what audiences want to see. The more energy and enthusiasm he has, the bigger the motor that drives his desire to learn his craft and develop that craftsmanship to a point of artistry. He suddenly realizes in common place objects and situations, characteristics and aspects which he was totally unaware of before. The uncreative man is one-sided. He develops his potentialities along one line. The creative actor must be many-sided.

These qualities he possesses are what audiences want to see—portraying with empathy the characters with which they can identify. Audiences for stage, screen and television are composed of those who have not fully developed their own desires. They depend on actors to vicariously fill this void. In times of grief and trouble, actors and entertainers have arrested time and diverted attention. They have given solace and relief from emotional tensions allowing subconscious minds to recharge and revitalize with new inspiration.

When a performance is sincerely communicated by the actor, it serves it's purpose well. It diverts the audience's attention and many times plugs them into an exciting emotional and spiritual experience, if only for a short time.

So if you want to be an actor, you certainly have your work cut out for you. Whether a beginner or a seasoned professional, Stanislavski says you must live the part each and every time you go on stage to portray a character.

You need to learn how to change your liabilities into assets and develop an exciting and arresting personality. You must also become interesting to look at physically. You must have power, balance, polarity, and you need to learn how to interweave your own personality with that of the character, with empathy to an audience—with impact.

You'll need to learn about common denominators and how to ask the "If" question. How to construct a physical structure to support and control the creation of your subconscious. Also, how to organize the machinery of the conscious mind so that it works with dependability every time, growing an ever enlarging tap root, directly to your subconscious for new thoughts and ideas. These new thoughts are inspiration, and *controlled inspiration is creation*! Eventually you will gain confidence that your supply of inspiration is greater than your demand. You'll have faith in your ability to supply more than is ever needed.

You will experience the gratification of good taste, as you choose and select that which is best for you; After developing good taste you will become exhilarated and exciting. When you're excited there is no time for boredom. Polarize the sensation of boredom; this is what your audience has not been able to do. But, thank God for the vast majority of people who are your audience. Without them your services wouldn't be needed.

You have a chance to go all the way, from Home Town, U.S.A. to international stardom! How quickly you get there, if you get there, depends on *how well* you understand the material presented here. Stardom depends on a sense of values and your enthusiasm. Develop the habit of enthusiasm by becoming spontaneously curious. Find out all you can about everything you can. Start with the book you are holding in your hands. What is the title, who is the author? Who is the publisher, what color is it, how much did it cost? Are you willing to pay the real price of becoming a professional actor and if so why?

There aren't any "short-cuts." It's a process that you must go through. You must let the process work. If you'll apply this formula to common place objects and situations around you, you'll develop new enthusiasm for your everyday surroundings. They will take on added significance, with interesting dramatic qualities. You'll respond to them intellectually and emotionally.

A lot of this may not mean very much to you now, but *it will* later...much more later. You should be proud of yourself for taking a chance. For making a commitment to make yourself the best possible *you*. It takes dedication and faith. Keep the faith in you heart, and your mind will become aware of what you can do. Then, you will truly understand.

You will understand that there are basic laws governing acting as in every aspect of life. Learn to work within the framework of these natural laws and the sky's the limit. But if you break one of these laws, you'll watch your portrayal self-destruct before your eyes and your audience.

Do your *best* with every exercise, every performance you're called upon to do. If you sincerely do the best you're capable of, then you'll live up to the hereditary tradition of your fellow actors and acting.

The time-tested truths present here are comprehensive, functional and effectively laid out for your consideration and ease of comprehension. They are the basic foundations, laws, and techniques of acting for anyone who wants to communicate with power and impact. Most of the great actresses that I know refer to themselves as "actors." Robert Mitchum, great film star, once said "Actor, actress what's the difference?" Marlo Thomas considers herself a pretty fair actor, and so do I!

When I use the term "actor," I am also referring to the actress.

CHAPTER TWO

Your Problems
(Are My Business)

Welcome to boot camp. This boot camp is for actors in all phases of the entertainment industry and was developed over the past century by the greatest teachers, coaches, directors, producers, and actors of our time or any other time. This material was developed and added on to in an ascending spiral to its present day state of realism. There is a Latin proverb that translates, "Though we are all made of clay, a bowl is not a vase. That is so true, but the actor must try."

The actor who recognizes and accepts the concrete scientific principles that rule the art can use them to observe reality and translate-through his voice, mind and body, these observations. He can apply these translations to words written by someone else, under direction conceived by someone else, and under conditions supplied by some one else.

The actor's problems are my business. I must continually keep myself aware of changes in "style" and cycles that demand change by the public. I continually stay up with where jobs are most plentiful for actors. Then I must teach the actor the know-how to get and hold these jobs. Jobs are more plentiful now than ever before, as films, television, and other projects burn up material and talent at a rapid-fire pace! It's an on-going problem of finding new talent to fill these positions.

The audience has lots of experience in putting the actor under a "microscope," through the mediums of the spotlight and the close-up. It can look intimately into the actor's eyes, watch each subtle movement and believe him or not. The audience is well trained at listening, as well as knowing instinctively, that there is something more to a voice than just what it hears. Remember, when you hear in "real life," you're listening in stereo and seeing in three dimensions. But, as a famous drama coach, now deceased, used to always remind me, the microphone has only *one ear* and the camera *one eye*. The audience knows that there is another quality in a voice or picture that causes him or her to "feel," to actually trigger an experience and cause him or her to like or dislike the actor. These are only two areas in which an actor can develop an added "extra something," or "edge," that gives impact and excitement to his personality and performance. Two developments very important to the film actor are enlarged screens and electronic advances in sound systems. I tell you this now so you'll know why we go through the eye and facial exercises and all the vocal calisthenics.

Imagine an actor with a chronic nervous twinge or a non-stop blinker, or an actor with a pair of wild eyebrows whipping across the end of a theater. On a large screen in a movie theater, a one-half inch lift of an eyebrow can mean an elevation of ten feet. Or what if an actor had no control over any of the twenty-three sets of muscles in the face?

The actor's job, along with being in complete control of his voice, body, and mind, is to "give the audience the truth!"

The professional actor has here a refresher with which to stay in "tone." The recruit in this boot camp is being indoctrinated in his basic training. (It will take you eight weeks or more to begin to get this material down.) The raw recruit is gaining self-knowledge as well as working toward his immediate goal, building the tools and laying the foundation of an acting career.

While the successful actor acquires prestige and social standing in plying his well-paid profession, it may take an average of five or six years to establish himself to the point of rising above or surviving a bad show, lifting a fair one above mediocrity, and always enhancing a good one by his very presence. But you must have complete control over every aspect of your actor's instrument.

If you want to live your *own* life, don't become an actor. As an actor you will have to live the life that will be best for you. Also, you will have *one* final source of authority to determine what that best is. You'll have to leave the trends to the masses, the crowds, which will be your audience. You'll have to get the clothes that enhance your career, not a weird assortment of faddish and trendy things. You'll have to get the hairstyle and haircut that will get you the job.

The nucleus of the actor's career is made up of highly skilled and competent specialists. "No one single person ever makes an actor," is a Hollywood axiom. Many people have a hand in creating him, from the very spirit and substances inherent in him.

The teachers, coaches, agents, publicists, and personal managers play important parts to be sure. But the make-up department, wardrobe department, sound and lighting engineers are just as important to the actor's career as the producer, director, and cutter. The head electrician you will discover is just as much a specialist in his field as the writer. These people know how to show the actor off to his best advantage. They are not prejudiced by personal whim. They arrive at their decisions in workman-like cooperation, functioning in a chain of command, that goes link by link to the top.

At the top is a single source of authority that must be the lode star of the actor's faith.

After faith is awareness and after that is understanding. If you are to fulfill your purpose, you must go through this "boot camp." Just keep in mind that every star in New York, Los Angeles, Dallas, or any where else, went through the exact same thing you're going through now.

Make the commitment and stick to "your guns and God," and let go completely until you have absorbed the entire material here. Then, and only then, can you evaluate it intelligently. Accept it, or reject it, in whole or in part. Then you will have earned the right to your own decision. I will guide you toward the threshold of a successful career, but you will have to cross that threshold and take the final steps yourself. On your own.

CHAPTER THREE

Impact
(And How Energy Creates It)

An actor must *fascinate* his audience! During the process of developing individualism and daring, it is important to use *good taste* as a control. I'm not encouraging you to become a "character." Hollywood and New York are full of actors (characters) who have a false opinion of their own importance. They're usually out on the "fringe edge," and they give away their exaggerated, distorted evaluations of themselves, by voices a little too loud, hair worn a little too long, or too short, shoulders a little too padded t-shirts and jeans a little too tight or too torn—and wisecracks that aren't quite funny. They are indeed characters, but not individualists. They're not even good copyists.

Balance, polarity, and poise must come into play. One of the greatest actors of our time is Marlon Brando, who for a long, long time has had a brilliant career and is an outstanding individualist. In his prime he was a serious student and practitioner of his art. He approached his craft with a combination of great daring and deep humility. He had no fear of being ridiculed, when as a top ranking star, he went back to his coach and worked for many months more perfecting his craft. "A pretty good actor will rehearse a scene a couple of hundred times," my coach used to say, "and a Brando will do it a thousand times."

Never let fear win out. Take a chance. Tear down your fear of absurdity. When asked to "stand up and say a few words," accept and do your best. Next time you'll do better. There's one comforting thought, if someone else could do better, they would be where you are and you would be in the audience. Remember most of the people listening can't do so well.

Whenever I found myself faced with an ordeal like giving a book report or junior speech making, my mother used to always say, "What have you got to be afraid of? Your friends and family will be proud of you and you don't know the other people, so what difference does it make?" I always had faith in her principles and theories, and they always worked. Where did she come up with these theories? From her mother, my grandmother, passed down from generation to generation.

Unerring truths. Unchangeable and unaltered by time. As valid now as they were then.

Don't let your vast reservoir of energy be held back by boredom or boring people. Bored people are tired people. People without vitality are never very interesting.

If an actor is exciting and interesting, he cannot be bored or boring. To prove my point, in class one day, it seemed as if the students would all fall asleep any second. I asked "Why are you all so tired and lifeless today?" Of all the excuses you could ever imagine, I got them all. My baby kept me up last night, I had a toothache, I didn't get any sleep and so forth. So, I said "Elvis Presley is coming over here for a private lesson in less than an hour from now. I thought you might like to stay and meet him, but since you're all so tired, you might as well go on home. Well! I have never seen people's countenance lift so quickly and attitudes change. All of a sudden, no one was tired any more!

All people have within them an almost unlimited supply of energy dammed up and choked off by mental and emotional barriers—most of which they aren't even aware of. Whether you realize it or not, the energy is there—more of it than you'll ever need.

Dynamic and creative men and women in all fields have learned to tear out the barriers that hold back their great storehouses of energy. Once you learn to tap this reservoir of energy, you will become a vital, creative actor with power and drive.

There are many psychological reasons for the barriers you've built, which stifle your energy, but for our purposes you only need to focus on two of these barriers. Fear of absurdity and boredom.

A swollen ego, which is really a *superiority complex*, but usually referred to as an *inferiority complex*, is usually the root cause. We cannot stand to be laughed at or not come in first or not be best. We must always win. We must rid ourselves of this fear of absurdity just as we would a bad tooth.

There are many ways to rid yourself of this barrier to your goal. One way is to say to yourself "Win, lose, or draw. So what!"

Remember you're going to become a daring individual because you *must* to be an actor. If you think you are being asked to make a fool of yourself in anything you are doing, in preparation or performance of a role—do it anyway, as long as you stay within the bounds of good taste.

Take a chance. Like Brando, be fearless now, as you begin to fit the mold! The actor's mold of making the audience "feel" and giving a convincing performance. Your audience will be amazed at you and filled with admiration—perhaps even envy.

The actor must be an individualist, perhaps more than any other creative artist in any other field. It is the individualism that makes him stand out from the average man and woman. But while you are giving expression to your individualism, don't forget to be humbly grateful. Thank your lucky stars that the world is populated by average people because they are your audience. They have the same unexpressed desires, unattained goals, and unrelieved scales of feelings that exist in the characters of plays, novels, and films. When empathy is created between the actor and the audience, they are able to expose their desires, attain their goals, and relieve their feelings.

Some of the first exercises I'll give you may seem somewhat strange or silly to you, but believe me there is a good reason for each and every one of them. An actor must keep his mind and body alert and vital. He doesn't have time for boredom. I repeat, a bored person is a tired person and a tired person is dull and unexciting. An actor must be an exciting personality!

I'm going to ask you to practice various exercises for a few minutes at a time. My purpose is to keep you from becoming bored. By giving you new and different trains of thought to follow at properly spaced intervals, I will help you retain enthusiasm in your approach to a very complex subject, and thus help forestall the frustrations that could hold you back.

Extending this principle into general living, it's important to give yourself a vast variety of diversions and interests. They allow your subconscious to renew your imagination, so you can return to your vocation—the building of an acting career—with constantly renewed enthusiasm!

You should have at least one or two hobbies. This will help you retain your singleness of purpose in constructing a solid career as an actor.

Most of the people I come into contact with are stimulating individuals, with at least two or three hobbies.

I feel it's my responsibility to make my clients aware of the many exciting activities and ideas going on in the world. I encourage them to keep several projects going all the time. The result is they don't have time to get bored or fatigued.

My own interests are a widely assorted range of activities with a definite aim of doing something which has little if anything to do with my actual work as a teacher of actors. I find that my hobbies, far from interfering with my career, help me do a full day's work, at my top level of efficiency. If you want to get something done, find the busiest person to do it.

When I get tired, I sometimes head out to a horse stable. I might go for a ride or just climb up on a fence rail and talk to some of the friendly cowboy types I find there. If time doesn't permit me to leave the studio, I'm happy to look through some horse magazines, and before long I'm ready to return to work with a renewed and rested mind and body. I enjoy art and visiting art galleries and always keep an easel with oil paints and a few canvasses in different stages of completion. I also enjoy going out and sketching old barns and run-down, falling-down old farm houses. I always take my camera and like to take pictures, too.

A well educated person who is widely informed, through a variety of activities, can become *aware* of many things he was unaware of before. When you get several projects going, your scope will broaden. You'll be more interesting to people. You will find yourself becoming an educated person. You will find yourself developing enthusiasm. *Interest creates enthusiasm—enthusiasm releases energy*!

Whatever you do in life, whether an actor, brick mason, business man, or president of Nuclear Energy, Inc., you'll be more exciting if you can train yourself to use this formula as one of your *musts* in your daily life.

CHAPTER FOUR

Fitting the Mold
(Let Yourself Go)

W e have said that you must be a disciplined individual with faith and patience, to become a good actor. Some questions you may want to ask yourself are: When a performance on stage or film is pleasing, does it make you wish you were that actor? Do you ever feel lonely in a large crowd? Do you ever feel unusually friendly in a large crowd? Do you sometimes get very happy when you are alone? Do you sometimes get very blue when you are alone? When a performance is funny or sad, do you laugh or cry easily? Do you have strong desires? When you are happy, are you *very* happy? When you were a child did you like to make-believe? When you are anxious are you very anxious? When you are angry are you very angry?

Have you always wanted to act? Do you daydream? Do you have faith in yourself?

If you answered yes to most of these questions, chances are that your emotional scale is flexible and potentially broad and that you have some of the basic material you'll need for an acting career.

I was asked these very same questions when I first started studying acting in Hollywood in the 1950's with a very famous drama coach. He had been under contract to most of the major studios and taught and developed the careers of the greatest stars in the business from Shirley Temple to Lucille Ball, from Gregory Peck to Clark Gable. I started studying along side many famous names in show business, and it helped me immensely. I studied for five years and served as my drama coach's assistant teacher for three more years.

I could see that my real interest was in developing actors and teaching talent. Exploring the mental and physical apparatus of the voice, mind, and body and making advances in the science underlying the art of acting and directing became my goal. After going through boot camp (just as you are) and building the basic foundation, I began years of study into the mechanics and underlying superstructures and tools of the art. I discovered many truths, but one of the most fascinating discoveries I made was that just as in building a character, you should always develop yourself to your highest and best use. This encompasses many of the problems the actor has. After many years as an actor and dramatic coach in the television and motion picture businesses I found my highest and best use was in teaching actors to become exciting personalities through the techniques I had learned. Developing natural God-given gifts and advantages and abilities in actors to their highest and best use was my calling and is my calling. How to become a craftsman and possess the know-how to develop that craftsmanship into a dependable set of actor's tools. To help forge the keys that open the doors to utilize all of your potentialities in a scientific manner, through the use of the time-tested truths I've mentioned. We are going to put these laws in cement and obey them always, as they will not ever change or let you down.

You want to know how to start, what to do and how to go about doing it. It's often been said "All the world's a stage." Let's find out something about how to act on it.

CHAPTER FIVE

Stair Steps to Stardom
(Put One Foot In Front Of The Other)

Some very important self-discoveries are awaiting you. Some surprises, a few shocks, but most of all a sense of authority will begin to show through and develop as you progress.

You will be more interesting.

You will be more attractive.

You will be more masculine if you are a man.

You will be more feminine if you are a woman.

You will add to your natural charm.

You will add to your natural abilities.

You will both feel and reveal added vitality.

You will establish and justify new self-confidence.

You will develop your character, dependability, and perseverance.

Your first impressions on other people will change considerably for the better.

You will broaden your horizons.

You will speak better.

You will project new power.

You will have a stronger personality.

You will gain poise.

You will know how to concentrate.

You will be able to think on your feet.

You will find out everything about yourself—your strengths and weakness can be used to your advantage.

Stardom is made of many steps, and you start by putting one foot in front of the other.

After acquiring self-knowledge and training under expert guidance, you'll learn to stylize your liabilities into assets and to develop your natural assets into symbols of an ideal.

The actor must have such control, such technique (know-how) that he can quickly and accurately give the director, camera man, and cutter what he needs and the audience what it wants.

What is acting? Webster's Dictionary says that to act is "to produce an effect." To produce an effect upon the emotions of the audience is the aim of every actor.

What is the actor's starting point? You start with every great actor's three fundamental laws:

- The Law of Faith.

- The Law of Awareness.

- The Law of Understanding.

Apply these laws right now:

- Have faith in me.

- You will become aware of what you can do.

- Then you will understand how to build and use the tools of acting.

How do you act?

You act by using the three primary elements upon which all acting is based:

- The voice

- The body

- The mind

These are the materials that go into your acting. These are the tools of your craft. They are the eloquent instrument of your art.

The voice and the body must be made so flexible that they will instantly obey the commands of the mind without conscious effort.

26

You need to be able to identify exactly *what* you need to become even better than you are. Always keep the windows of your mind open to new ideas, concepts, and techniques.

You're already special. You're in the small minority of people that realize that the acting profession requires constant study, review, and practice. Now if you think that's not special, look around you. Look at the ordinary actor and what he's doing. You are investing the time and energy to seek answers and new insights, and you'll find them.

Ask yourself these three important questions:

How can I use this concept?

How can I use these ideas?

How can I use these techniques?

Don't ever stop digging for ideas to help you grow. Don't start coasting, mistaking the beachhead for the island of success.

Acting is a science that requires hard work and dedication. When you approach your work in this manner the results become predictable.

How much time have you spent on your acting career? All professionals spend time preparing themselves. Most public speakers spend about five hours in preparation for every one hour in front of their audience. Lawyers can spend up to thirty hours preparing for every one hour in front of the jury. Advertising people spend about 150 hours or more preparing the materials that go into a thirty second television spot. Yet one recent study showed that the average beginning actor spent less than an average of thirty minutes a day preparing for his career.

After you have prepared and have an excellent knowledge of your craft, you will be extremely well qualified to present it. You will find out that acting is a *learned* skill. You weren't born knowing how to act, but by applying certain principles, presented here, it will all come together.

Because you are approaching your career as a professional, it's important to know what stage of development you're in now as well as where to set your goal.

To become a capable craftsman, you will need to be a *conscious, unconscious, competent*. Knowing that you know, doing what you know, but doing it automatically without even thinking about it and repeating your performance time after time with success. This permits you to be totally flexible and personalize each character.

When you watch a great actor on stage or in motion pictures, he or she actually becomes the person they're playing. They're natural and spontaneous. You know there's a script, rehearsals, and many hours of preparation and takes involved, but when the audience sees it, it's real!

On the other hand, when you watch a John Wayne movie, one of over 200 he made (with great professionalism, I might add), was he a great actor?

In every film he ever made, who was he? John Wayne!

In the ring a fighter reacts not through instinct but through training.

When you watch a great dancer, athlete, or musician, what they're doing may appear very natural and spontaneous, but each is a highly trained professional who has spent endless long hours in preparation.

Does this effort and energy pay off? You bet it does!

Danny DeVito was called by everyone "the funny little man." Danny had a philosophy and a plan. "It's what's inside your head that counts," he said. "It's your goal and your knowledge that are critical." In 1986 he was competing with over 25,000 other actors. The average earnings of all Screen Actors Guild actors was under $3,600.00 for that year. In 1986 Danny DeVito earned over $5 million dollars. There's only one question on his mind when talking to producers, directors and casting people: "When do I start?"

CHAPTER SIX

Technique
(Know-How)

Y ou begin with the physical apparatus: arms—
legs torso—tongue—eyes—facial muscles and
so on from skeleton to skin.

Technique is mechanics.

Technique is the foundation of acting.

The tallest skyscraper in the world would collapse and fall without a solid foundation. It is impossible to give great performances on stage or in
film without one.

The fast paced world of television especially
demands solid mechanical supports. When shoot-
ing the same lines time after time, you must be a
capable craftsman with a solid foundation before
you can begin to flood and color a role with your
own personality. You may think this all sounds

very mechanical and it is, but you must have at your command, ready to serve you, at your director's will—a practical knowledge of the mechanics of acting.

The seven tones of the musical scale are mechanical too, but they can be used artistically to produce and create a great piece of music. The three (3) primary colors and their divisions are mechanical, but they too may be selected and blended in such a way as to create a masterpiece. It is the framework that supports a piece of architecture that is artistic and inspiring in its finished form. A great tennis player doesn't start out by going onto the court and hitting the ball over the net. It is not until he has bounced the ball against the wall several thousand times and learned how to hold the racket, how to bounce the ball, how to place his feet, and hands, his body, and so forth.

Do I believe in mechanical acting? No. But I believe an actor must build a solid mechanical mold before he can overcome hidden and obvious weaknesses. Among other shortcomings, it will lack continuity of line and above all *authority*. I believe this one word, *authority*, is one of the most important words to the actor and that this is accomplished by building a solid foundation, a good basic technical foundation that can be the deciding factor in whether you work—or not in the acting profession. Is it possible to give an inspired performance without technique? Yes—

but not night after night on the stage and time after time in film with all the deadlines and budgets to meet.

There are some inspired performances given all the time by inspired amateurs. Some are very effective, but those who give them can rarely duplicate their performances and then only by accident—because talented amateurs haven't developed their voice, body, or mind as dependable technical tools.

The important thing is to give an inspired performance. And, if you were to ask me "Do I need talent to be a working actor?" I would tell you "No." Many actors have made good livings by becoming such capable craftsmen, in their use of the tools of acting that they have overcome the handicap of not having native talent. They've made up for what they lack as inherent artists, by becoming highly skilled, superior artisans—experts in the mechanics of acting.

This soundly organized technique, for transmitting emotions, words, actions, and ideas to an audience, is craftsmanship at its best.

Technique is another word for know-how. There is *technique for everything* from baking a cake to moving a heavy piece of furniture, from the dentist drilling a tooth, to enacting a scene in a play. Your knowledge and appreciation of acting technique will give effective performance and help you find freedom of expression at any time under any circumstances.

Without technique there is no *control*. I repeat, you must have such control, such know-how— that you can quickly and accurately give each person in the *film crew what he needs* and *the audience what it demands!*

A good actor must excite an audience. He must be interesting to look at and pleasing to listen to, and he must be able to transmit these qualities with *impact*! A good actor must have polarity and balance.

Polarity is the quality of having opposite or contrasting poles of feeling. Happy—sad, black–white, day—night are all examples of polarity. Polarity is the basis of dramatic conflict. The skillful use of contrasting extremes enables an actor to project these extremes in the emotional scale and enables him to project these extremes with authority, while not actually experiencing them himself.

It is not an actor's job to "feel" per se, but to *make the audience feel* what is being transmitted to them. He or she can show anger, without being angry or depict love without being in love with his leading lady. A good actor can also portray pride without being in love with himself. To clinch the argument, an actor need not die to play a death scene! By using his thoroughly trained and well-developed poles of feelings, he can play on the emotions of the audience and make them feel they have seen someone die.

Balance means, "The ability to equalize or compensate," by offsetting one—factor against another. An actor establishes equality and achieves symmetry or balanced form. Through symmetry he gains form and poise. *Balance* is the key word to *poise*. Perfect balance between the desire to express and the ability to express contributes to poise. Once again, this requires the knowledge of technical tools.

The first problems are really quite simple. Things like how to stand, how to sit, what is good posture, and so forth.

Since acting is based on the three primary elements, the voice, the body and the mind, *thorough training* of each is a set requirement. You must chisel this in granite! It will never change!

These first exercises, such as how to exercise your face and eyes and coordination exercises, may seem easy.

You will be learning to always break down into units and objectives all of your character portrayals. We must go off the road at the right place or we would soon be hopelessly lost.

You may wonder what these simple exercises have to do with acting. Let me assure you, they have a great deal to do with acting.

If your physical apparatus is flexible, alert, and well enough controlled to obey the commands of your mind, your body will be able to do it's part in projecting thoughts and emotions, with or without dialogue.

Basic parts that add up to the sum total of the science underlying the art of acting. The technique, craftsmanship, mechanics, and know-how are what this boot camp is all about.

CHAPTER SEVEN

Look Like A Star!
(Look In The Mirror)

Have you ever noticed that when looking at a star, they can be standing, sitting, or lying down, but they all have the same thing, good posture (which is what I call the V-shape). It's time for you to start practicing how to sit, stand and walk (with impact!).

Imagine there is a hook fastened under you sternum (breast bone). It pulls your chest up and out. Your chest is high, your chin level, shoulders relaxed and slightly forward. (This adds about an inch to each side.) The old adage about the shoulders should be squared back is just another fallacy that we will be exposing. Your spine should be straight, your waist long—abdomen flat—buttocks pinched in and tucked under. Weight resting lightly on the balls of the feet—feet shoulder length apart for men—one step in for women. Now! That's good posture! (The V look) As a general rule to help you, the larger the base or further apart the feet of a man or woman generally indicates less intelligence. You could say the closer the base, the closer the feet are together, generally the more intelligent the person is. Take for instance, a drunk. His base would be far apart, and his walking would be sloppy. Once you have found the V shape, for the character, stay in the mold no matter what. Practice it daily every time you are standing or sitting.

Exercise

Assume the V shape and tighten every muscle in your body. Then still in position, relax as much as you possibly can without any collapse of the muscle structure.

In other words keep the same mold or position, but use an absolute minimum of tension to hold this mold. Repeat this exercise fifteen to twenty-five times a day, *every day*. Every time you do this, you're working in *relaxed constriction*. (The first of many keys you'll be forging.)

Relaxed constriction is *disciplined freedom*, or *controlled ease*. To experience this, put your arms between a doorway with palms toward your legs and push out with the back of your hands on the door jam for 30 seconds hard. When you walk away your arms tend to fly up, all by themselves. You can almost forget their existence. This is an example of *relaxed constriction* of *polarity*, the opposites (tension-relaxation also called isolation-relaxation) and of balance (the harmonious equalizing of these opposites).

To experience something is quite different than merely reading or talking about it. By going through the motions and actually experiencing relaxed constriction, you have begun to integrate its principles and practice into your very being.

Your new posture will develop rapidly as you use the principles of relaxed constriction. Always remember to fit movements into the V shape, as you practice daily. Keep in mind, as an actor you must look symmetrical and exciting.

Further experience in other phases of the mechanics that go into acting will help you make the technique of the art genuinely yours (a part of you).

To look like a star means balance, polarity, vitality, relaxed constriction, the V shape, and developing the mind picture. Every time you catch yourself out of the V shape, go back into it immediately by using the Law of Substitution.

Your stomach and midriff muscles may be a bit sore during the first few days of practice upon your posture hook, using relaxed constriction.

Let's imagine the hook under your sternum is fastened to an overhead traveler, that goes everywhere you do, pulling you up. Now, let's put that new posture into motion by walking.

When you walk, disturb as little air as possible and remember to use *economy of motion*, not only when you walk, but in all your acting movements.

Remember to make yourself long through the middle, keep your shoulders relaxed and slightly forward, suspend from your hook always. Let your arms do the work, not your shoulders. Alert your muscles for muscle tone and once again disturb as little air as possible.

I'll continue hammering away at you while you're in training in this boot camp and while I do, keep this in mind: There isn't a star in New York, Hollywood, Dallas, Chicago, or anywhere else, that hasn't gone through the same thing, you're going through now. Actors are diligent, hard working men and women. Even after years of rigorous training, they spend additional months of training to prepare themselves for every new role, remember stars weren't born stars, they became stars by paying the price.

One famous actor I work with takes each new script and after settling the subconscious and the conscious objectives of the character, he then creates (through relaxed constriction) a physical self, as well. I must stress the importance of these exercises, for they take base metals and return pure gold!

You'll need to have faith in my knowledge and experience and faith in yourself as well. Faith that you're creating a new and exciting you. The *real you* that God created.

CHAPTER EIGHT

A Mental Image
(Becomes Real)

Now, you're going to have to begin to be an observer of life. There was a time when actors were taught to pose in a particular way to depict grief, arch an eyebrow to portray doubt, and shift their weight from here to there to express haughtiness. That sort of thing has no place in the technique of today's enlightened actor. The emotional scale is not played by moving from one specific pose to another. Two actors don't portray sadness the same way. Or, for that matter the same way in two different characterizations. Take a look around you. At school, at a funeral, a wedding, an accident, a theater, or any place, you see that emotion is highly personal. It is intensely individualistic in its expression.

Since different people have different ways of expressing emotion, the actor must develop *understanding* as well as technical tools. This lends itself to flexibility and control, which will enable him to portray emotions in many different ways. The tools are the same for everyone. The end result of their use is individual.

After thorough training your voice and body will become so flexible and so well controlled that they will automatically obey the commands of the mind without conscious effort.

Any acting theory that cannot be proved and improved upon by actual use isn't any good. If it's excess baggage in the actor's tool kit. Get rid of it.

Bit by bit, step by step, the science underlying the actor's art will become concrete in concept, defined in detail, and clear in purpose to you. When it does, you will be able to use the science with personal selectivity and professional judgment, as do the great communicators of our time. We are all creatures of habit and have characteristics which influence our personality patterns.

Our own personalities are made up of habits, fears, gratification's, inhibitions, complexes, mannerisms, and traits which are, for the most part, subconscious.

We all know that there are two parts to the mind—the conscious and the subconscious. The conscious is your voluntary mind, your aware mind—the mind that functions when you're awake. The subconscious is your involuntary mind. It functions when you're asleep, as well as when you're awake. It functions all the time and has in it every single thing that you've ever seen, thought, heard, felt, or sensed in any way.

You can use your conscious and your subconscious mind as tools of acting to develop, heighten, and enhance your own personality.

Make *this* mental image. You are in a vast desert at night and you're lost. All you have is a flashlight and a horse. You and the horse you're on, can be compared to the size of your measurable, conscious mind—the vast unmeasured desert to your subconscious mind.

The subconscious desert conceals many things of which you are not aware, but they are there just the same...anything that you can think of is there, and everything that you have ever known is there.

A fraction of the vastness passes through your flashlight beam which we call the "aware beam." Beautiful cactus plants and flowers, rocks, and dangerous animals and snakes. Big and little habit patterns, fear and daring, destructive land mines— buried just beneath the sand. As some of these things pass through your flashlight beam, which once again we'll call your "aware beam," you can focus on them, to see something of what's going on down in your subconscious.

You can focus your "aware beam" on potentially dangerous things like deep hidden fears or on habits and personality mannerisms.

Let's say you've focused your "aware beam" on a dangerous land mine, barely sticking out of the sand (which is just a way of representing a potentially dangerous fear), as soon as the mine is in your "aware beam," it can be successfully dealt with.

You can pull it into your conscious mind, examine it, find its detonator and remove it. The fear then ceases and you can safely throw the pieces back into the desert sand, and they will sink harmlessly into your subconscious.

Or, let's say that your "aware beam" spots a bad habit such as poor posture, sloppy walking, or incorrect breathing. After you've focused on the bad habit, you can use what is called *the Law of Substitution*, to correct the bad habit by consciously constructing a new "good" habit to replace the old "bad" habit.

You can use the Law of Substitution in dealing with any undesirable trait by substituting good traits and habits for old traits and bad habits.

While bad habits, fears, and undesirable personal traits, are within your "aware beam," you may know they're there—and yet refuse to recognize them. You figuratively hold your hand up in front of your eyes, like a blinder, to hide from yourself whatever you don't want to see. We will refer to this as a hand-inhibition.

It's up to you to consciously dispense with your hand-inhibitions and look squarely at what is within focus of your "aware beam." By using the

Law of Substitution you can transform your liabilities into assets.

To get into the character's conscious and subconscious, the actor must use all the imagination and training at his command. The actor should represent the character's personality over his own. I always tell my students that it's more important to have the character's inner thoughts and personality down pat than his physical likeness.

Since all traits and habits, regarding the conscious and the subconscious are true of our own personalities in real life, it stands to reason that they should exist in every character an actor creates.

To ring true, a character's personality should be made up of habits, fear, gratifications, inhibitions, complexes, personality mannerisms, and so forth. These should consciously be built into the character's subconscious, by the actor.

This is creativity plus! This is natural and this rings true. Break the laws of nature and heaven help you.

By substituting the character's personality for his own, the actor establishes a *common denominator*, a bridge or *connector*, between an insulated image and an interpreted realism.

With the conscious-subconscious technique, you pull all the other elements along. Just as with the objective defined and the thought line clear and settled long before the director ever says "Action," the conscious-subconscious technique will

44

serve you well. That is as long as you enter into this threshold *naturally*.

Keep your self alert to the many uses of the *Law of Substitution*. It is within this law that an unfulfilled personality can be molded into an exciting star.

But, I repeat, without an indestructible inner urge, without great drive and desire, and singleness of purpose—no teacher in the world can change you into that exciting star you're striving to be.

The brightness and scope of each person's "aware beam" is in direct proportion to his intelligence. The greater the intelligence, the bigger the engine that drives and powers his desire to penetrate the subconscious and thus discover himself.

One of my students with this kind of drive has developed her facial expressions to the point of excellence. In a tight choker shot, her director said recently, "Her face is a dictionary of silent synonyms for actual words." Quite a complement from a director.

As you progress with the mechanical exercises, focus your "aware beam" on each new element we take up in the mechanics and science underlying the actor's art.

With renewed resolve start each day with positive affirmations and thoughts. These conscious thoughts positively control your destiny.

To help you learn you can always make use of these two important facts:

1. Your conscious self learns during periods of concentration.

2. Your subconscious learns during periods of relaxation.

Once you've absorbed all the terms and their meanings in this chapter, you'll be pleasantly surprised to find the added vitality you'll have.

Focus your "aware beam" on habit patterns, hand inhibitions, personality mannerisms, your conscious and subconscious mind, and *most importantly* don't forget to use the *Law of Substitution!* Your mental image of yourself *will* become the new you.

CHAPTER NINE

The Close-Up
(The Star Maker)

With a two hundred-fold to scale enlargement in mind, imagine whipping eyebrows. The audience would be so fascinated by the weird movements that they wouldn't be able to keep their minds on the dialogue.

Under the stimulation of excitement or dramatic tension, or from force of habit, eyebrows have a tendency to go wild.

Compare your own eyebrow acrobatics with any well-trained actor's close-up. There should never be excess movement of eye or brow to distract attention from expressions of emotions.

We all know people whose faces seem to have no vitality or tone. Their expressions are bloodless and flat. Organically these people may be healthy and yet give the impression of illness because there is no muscle tone or alertness in their faces.

After locating certain muscles with your mind you can develop the muscle tone for a healthy, vital, animated face.

Look in the mirror and locate the small muscles just under the lower eye-lids. Focus your "aware beam" on them until you can move them with conscious effort. At first your movements will be very broad. After exercising these lower eye-lid muscles you will develop amazing control. You'll be able to make the movements delicately and the motion itself will hardly be noticeable, but its effect will. Because of the thought process going on, mentally you will begin to use these muscles subconsciously, as well as consciously. Who will ever forget the subtle styling of Humphrey Bogart and the lower eye lid movement he stylized?

From almost invisible muscular movement comes that exciting, subtle play around the eyes. It's just a bit more technique that will help you characterize certain parts.

The smaller the muscular motion of the muscles, the more impact they have in their effect. The uncontrolled broad movement is a tool of the "ham." Once in a while it's fun to be a great big "ham"— but the actor who knows how to slice it, is the one who gets the best results, the greatest rewards, and the deepest satisfaction.

In motion pictures and television, where camera close-ups sometimes come within a few inches of the face, the importance of the eye cannot be overemphasized.

The actor should do everything he can to improve the use of the eyes and to increase their flexibility and control, until they become manageable tools of his trade.

The actor's eyes should be so revealing in their range of expression that the audience can read the thoughts of a character created by a performer.

The eyes have often been called the mirror of the soul because they reflect inner feelings. I often tell my students that I must see their eyes as they are the "entrance to their soul."

Learning to relax the eyes can be as important a tool as how to use them. Working with high wattage lights and powerful reflectors on sound stages for hours at a time, it becomes mandatory that you learn how to revitalize and relax the eyes.

Remember the physiology book in school with its picture of the eye, along with the muscles and nerves behind it? The muscles bunch-up and come together in a sort of knot just behind the eye ball. The point of relaxation is right there, where the muscles bunch up.

Close your eyes for a few minutes. Locate the "muscle knot" behind each eye with your mind (and do them one eye at a time). Imagine you are relaxing that knot behind the eye and that they will soon become relaxed. They have no choice at all. *The mind controls the body*. Also relax the blue veins at the temple and alongside the nose and the muscles around the mouth. Keep this on tap in your memory file, especially for motion pictures and television. With your well-trained and developed power of concentration, you can close your eyes lightly for a moment or two just before going in front of the camera to play a scene. When you reopen them they'll be relaxed and fresh, even after ten or twelve hours under bright studio lights.

Here is an exercise to develop control and flexibility of the eyebrows.

Exercise
(Repeat 15-25 times daily)

Slowly arch your eyebrows—as high as you can—slowly return to normal—then slowly pull the eyebrows down and together as close as you can in a frown—then return to normal.

All exercises should be practiced slowly under conscious physical control.

Focus your "aware beam" on the close-up—your close-up.

We're all familiar with the poker face and the overactive face. A poker face is all right for playing poker, and an overactive face is fine for the life-of-the party. But neither are of much help to the serious actor. A poker face transmits nothing at all and an overactive face soon becomes a meaningless blur. Training the facial muscles to respond on command is mandatory. It can be done, as many stroke and accident victims have discovered. Some truly heroic feats have happened from time to time when paralyzed people have located certain muscles with their mind. Recently one man I heard about was paralyzed from the neck down. He was able to mentally locate the muscle in one of his big toes, and that was his starting point. By starting there he was soon able to walk again.

There are many facial muscles which you can train physically after you have located them mentally. Some of your facial exercises will also help you overcome the fear of absurdity.

Touch the tip of your nose with your upper lip.

Don't cheat yourself by trying to push the upper lip with your jaw, lower lip or tongue.

Sit in front of a mirror and study the muscles which control the movements of your upper lip as you work it up and down. Try this exercise using the elevator muscles at the point of the cheek bones to lift the upper lip.

Exercise
(Repeat 15-25 times daily)

1. Use the elevator muscles on the right side of the lips; show the teeth.

2. Repeat for the left side.

3. Alternate these actions.

Now push both lips out as far as you can in a whistling position, at the same time locate the muscles that control the movement. You'll find them completely surrounding the lips.

Command these various muscles to perform for you, and they will!

Next try to turn your lip inside out. It's surprising how many "stiff upper lips" there are. Yet, for natural expression and to get equality and firmness of diction, you need to overcome that stiffness and acquire flexibility and control of the upper lip.

Without flexibility the mouth cannot be relaxed and natural for speech. Without control, it will move too much and in the wrong way. Imagine mouthings that are noticeable in the normal size. Now, imagine them in Cinemascope, VistaVision, Cinerama and all the rest of the gigantic, colossal and super systems for film projection.

A flexible upper lip will keep your face youthful. One of the first signs of age is losing the upper lip. With a flexible upper lip you can develop a relaxed smile.

In motion pictures and television the whites of the eyes, like the whites of the teeth, are of utmost importance. These whites reflect light which the camera picks up.

Study close-ups of top ranking motion picture and television players. Count off in mind exactly how long they hold their eyes perfectly still, without blinking or moving. Then consciously measure your own eye flexibility and control against theirs.

Here is an exercise to help you eliminate this weakness.

Exercise
(Repeat 15-25 times)

Concentrate on the elevator muscles at the point of the cheekbone. Contract and release these muscles. Try for independent muscular control. Don't close you eyes or even squint as you contract the muscles. Always keep in mind that these mechanized exercises serve very important *specific* purposes!

Our next exercise is Smile up—Smile down. This exercise was used by a famous cowboy actor I coached in preparation for almost every part he's ever portrayed. It's a dual purpose exercise as most of the exercises are that you'll be doing. He starts off with a broad smile as he slowly descends the staircase, one stair at a time. With this full smile, he slowly descends the staircase and realizes that he has been "hood-winked"—his smile goes down in exactly the same scale patterns of the stairs. When he gets to the bottom of the stairs he starts back up, and as he gets back up the stairs his smile comes back up into a full smile up. This simple exercise received rousing applause at a Hollywood premier of the film he was starring in—he had learned an object lesson in the importance of dependable technical resources, or tools. This exercise will give you the same results.

1. It develops muscle tone and flexibility.

2. It is an emotional "scale."

3. It helps develop the line of concentration.

Exercise

Sit comfortably in a chair and mechanically force the broadest "vaudeville" smile you possible can, stretching every muscle in your face. Show you teeth to the utmost.

Hold that smile for an instant, then slowly— ever so slowly, you can hardly feel the movement. Let go of the muscles holding the smile. Slowly let the smile and the energy that it takes to hold it up go down, all the way down—down until you almost break into a sob.

Just before you break into a sob, let the energy return gradually and slowly—slowly go back up. Eventually all the way back up to the high, forced, mechanical smile.

It should take about a minute to go down and the same amount of time to return to the original smiling position.

In the beginning the muscles in your face will jump and quiver during these *facial* calisthenics. Soon, you'll be able to blend smoothly the muscles used in going from the top to the bottom to the top. Add another control factor—imagination, and make it a dual purpose exercise. Imagine a story. The story has a happy beginning, gradually descending through conflicting moments of doubts and hopes until it sinks into a hopeless tragedy. Just before you break into a sob, you realize the whole thing must be a mistake—oh, yes, it is all a misunderstanding. Your hope gradually rises until you reach your original point of happiness. When you have completed this two-minute exercise several times, you will find that the physical action scale and the emotional scale *synchronize* and *support* each other, if they are controlled under strongly disciplined concentration.

When you are at the bottom of the emotional scale, your breathing is heavy and labored.

Your heartbeat is slow and loud. As you come back up with the emotional scale, you can feel your breathing and heartbeats speed up.

The effect is highly dramatic as you have seen this exact same exercise in the films of virtually every exciting star.

The glorious emotional color palette of a great actor is the benchmark with which to judge your progress. You really will be amazed at how quickly your emotional scale will develop, especially if you remember this: *"The greatest economy of movement always creates the greatest impact!"*

In an ever increasing competitive acting field, it's going to take all the extra "edges" you can add to your performance to get the job.

Don't worry about it; by the time you've mastered the material here, you'll be able to compete with anyone anywhere.

Keep the faith—faith that what you're doing is right and stay enthused and you will win at each and every phase of life.

CHAPTER TEN

The Laws of Timing
(Just Being Natural)

Y ou'll never have to ask this question again—
"What should I do with my hands?"

People completely fill a pause with movement, or they exactly synchronize speech with movement because they're doing what comes naturally. Their dialogue is spontaneous conversation, created under real-life conditions. Consciously or subconsciously, they direct their own scenes, in situations and sittings they predetermine.

The actor must speak dialogue created by someone else. He does it under conditions deliberately created by someone else, and he is directed by someone else. In other words, it's not real life. The source of what he has to say and do, when,

56

where, and how he has to say and do it, is outside his control.

When people move during a spoken phrase in real life, they generally start moving on the first syllable of the phrase and stop moving on the last syllable.

By watching others in natural conversations, we find them using these over-all speech-movement patterns. Instinctively, they are obeying two sets of laws. The first set is: *The Laws of Timing* which are the patterns codified and organized.

Notice these two patterns. When actors move during a pause (while not talking), the movement doesn't overlap either the end of their last spoken phrase or the beginning of their next spoken phrase. They will pause to take a breath and sometimes to emphasize certain words. The *pause*, as you will discover, is one of the most *powerful* tools the actor has.

The actor's problem is to make what he says and does, when, where, and how he says and does it, seem real, as if *he* were the source.

The actor's solution to that problem is the use of *common denominators*, or *connectors*. One tremendously important common denominator to help in his substitution of a character's personality for his own, is the dual pattern of speech and movement.

There are two times people move. When they're talking and when they are not talking.

This pattern becomes the formula of the *two Laws of Timing*.

First Law of Timing: Movement during a pause. Move during the *whole* pause and nothing but the pause.

Second Law of Timing: Movement during the vocal phrase. Move during the *whole* phrase and nothing but the phrase.

Start the movement on the first syllable of the first word in the phrase and end the movement on the last sound in the last syllable of the phrase.

Now that you've focused your "aware beam" on the two laws of timing as a connector and common denominator between acting and real life, *burn them into your conscious mind*!

Let's start with the eyes, face, arms, and hands in some single actions you make everyday. We will arbitrarily use them in some flexibility and control exercises.

Before you start your first flexibility exercise, sit down in a comfortable chair and look straight front. I will assume you are still on your posture hook.

Imagine your head completely filling a motion picture screen, with your nose at dead center. Your chin touches the bottom of the screen and the crown of your head touches the top.

Mentally pinpoint your nose at dead center by picking a spot on the wall in front of you, or by tacking a spot at nose dead center. Don't let the pull of gravity draw your head down, thereby dragging your nose below dead center. Don't let your head tilt or drift to one side.

In practicing this exercise, follow the numbered order of the units of motion.

You're establishing a technique habit of making one clean unit of motion.

Do each unit of motion to a count of four. If you are not in class, you can use a tape recorder to prerecord the drill for yourself. If you have no outside assistance, call the drill mentally as you do it. Be sure your eyes move in *clean. straight line*.

All right, head-on close-up. Nose dead center. Let's go:

Exercise
(Repeat 15-25 times)

1. Eyes right
2. Eyes center
3. Eyes left
4. Eyes center
5. Eyes up
6. Eyes center
7. Eyes down
8. Eyes center
9. Eyes right oblique up
10. Eyes center
11. Eyes left oblique up
12. Eyes center
13. Eyes right oblique down
14. Eyes center
15. Eyes left oblique down
16. Eyes center

In your next exercise while still completely filling your imaginary motion picture screen with your head and still keeping your nose pin-pointed at dead center, make—*separately* some eye and head movements. Make them without moving the shoulders or any other part of the body not specifically mentioned in the drill.

No drift.

At eyes right, for instance, focus your eyes on a definite point at your far right. Get your point and hold that point until you get another (eye order).

Take four counts for each single unit of motion and take the units in numerical order. The center of the screen is always your center in the exercise.

Exercise
(Repeat 15-25 times)

1. Eyes right
2. Nose right
3. Eyes center
4. Nose center
5. Eyes left
6. Nose left
7. Eyes center
8. Nose center
9. Eyes up
10. Nose up
11. Eyes center
12. Nose center
13. Eyes down
14. Nose down
15. Eyes center
16. Nose center
17. Eyes right oblique up
18. Nose right oblique up
19. Eyes center
20. Nose center
21. Eyes left oblique up
22. Nose left oblique up
23. Eyes center
24. Nose center
25. Eyes right oblique down
26. Nose right oblique down
27. Eyes center
28. Nose center
29. Eyes left oblique down
30. Nose left oblique down
31. Eyes center
32. Nose center

OK, now you're ready to add other arbitrary units of motion to this exercise. The first motion is a full smile. When the drill calls for "smile up," it means show your molars and hold the smile without drift, until you get a further smile order. "Smile down" means simply no smile. It doesn't have anything to do with frowning or making a grimace. The other units of motion use the hands and arms, but not the shoulders. This exercise is called a *"continuity cavalcade."* Follow the units of motion in numerical order.

Still seated comfortably and on your posture hook, look straight ahead. Rest both hands on your knees in a starting position.

Exercise
(Repeat 15-25 times)

1. Eyes center
2. Eyes left
3. Left hand to top shirt button
4. Smile up
5. Nose left
6. Right hand to top shirt button
7. Left hand down
8. Eyes center
9. Smile down
10. Nose center
11. Left hand to top shirt button
12. Eyes left oblique
13. Right hand down
14. Smile up
15. Nose left oblique up
16. Left hand down
17. Smile down
18. Eyes center
19. Right hand to top shirt button
20. Nose center
21. Right hand down

22. Eyes right oblique down
23. Left hand to top shirt button
24. Smile up
25. Nose right oblique down
26. Right hand to top shirt button
27. Eyes center
28. Smile down
29. Right hand down
30. Nose center
31. Eyes right oblique up
32. Left hand down
33. Right hand to top shirt button
34. Nose right oblique up
35. Smile up
36. Left hand to top shirt button
37. Eyes center
38. Nose center
39. Left hand down
40. Smile down
41. Right hand down
42. Relax

You have just completed an exercise using arbitrarily selected units of motion ... a whole procession of them ... a continuity cavalcade.

Practice this exercise until each independent unit of motion follows the other with clock-like precision. There must be absolutely *no overlap* between units. No drifting, squirming, or giggling-before, during, or after the units of motion.

It may take a few days to get the precise perfection of custom-made machinery, but they will be interesting days. Days of very important achievement!

You'll be able to use these tools you've just made automatically on command. They will become yours if you will but absorb them into your subconscious. Focus your "aware beam" on these arbitrary units of motion until they dissolve into your very being and then they will be yours to keep forever.

"To the winner goes the spoils; to the interceptor goes the touchdown." That's a fact of life, "So, run that you may obtain" (1 Cor. 9:24).

CHAPTER ELEVEN

The First Law of Timing
(Move During The Pause)

T he First Law of Timing is: Movement during
  the pause, the whole pause and nothing but
the pause.

We're going to focus our "aware beam" on the
First Law of Timing by doing an exercise scene
from Shakespeare's immortal "The Merchant of
Venice." An acting class wouldn't be complete
without Shakespeare.

We are using an excerpt from "Portia's trial
scene." Memorize the quotation word for word.
Get it perfect so you can rattle it off automatically.
Don't try to act it.

The Quality of Mercy Speech
(Memorize)

The quality of mercy is not strain'd,
It droppeth as the gentle rain from heaven
Upon the place beneath: it is twice bless'd;
It blesseth him that gives and him that takes:
'Tis mightiest in the mightiest; it becomes
The throned monarch better than his crown;
His septer shows the force of temporal power,
The attribute to awe and majesty,
Wherein doth sit the dread and fear of kings;
But mercy is above this scepter'd sway,
It is enthroned in the hearts of kings,
It is an attribute to God himself,
And earthly power doth then show likest God's
When mercy seasons justice.
Go through the speech again. This time notice that
   you automatically take pauses.

Breathe naturally in your pause. During each pause take only the breath you need to speak the vocal phrase comfortably which follows the breath. Keep going over the speech until it feels natural for you to breathe this way during your pauses. Repeat the speech and signal with your hand during each pause. Fill the complete pause with synchronized breathing and action.

Congratulations, you have just experienced our First Law of Timing.

First Law of Timing—movement during a Pause. Move during the whole pause and nothing but the pause. No overlap, this is *important!*

Now, obeying the First Law of Timing, do the "Quality of Mercy" speech, substituting one of our arbitrary units of motion, in place of the hand signal.

Again you have just experienced our First Law of Timing—plus the Law of Substitution, you have completely filled each pause with an action, but you have never overlapped action and speech.

This is the time to memorize a speech from a contemporary play, about the same length as "The Quality of Mercy" excerpt.

Take pauses in the new speech wherever they suit your interpretation. Only a director has the authority to change your pauses for the sake of overall interpretation, which is his responsibility. Once your pauses are set, however, make sure they are permanent and definably set. You have no right to change them. It is on your pauses that other actors, working with you, base their reactions. If you continually change your pauses, you become a difficult performer to work with. You would be totally unfair to your fellow actors.

After your pauses are "set" in the modern play speech, fill each pause with one of our arbitrary units of motion. Practice this until it becomes automatic.

Back to "The Quality of Mercy" speech, this time substituting a normal movement toward a normal body objective, such as taking off your jacket, use one single unit of motion in each pause.

Now, substitute the play speech for the "Quality of Mercy" speech and go through it with a normal body objective, such as taking off your jacket using one single unit of motion in each pause.

Let's see exactly what you've done in the last two speeches. Let's break down this business of objectives.

In almost every scene you play, there are usually two objectives.

First is the *speech objective*. You reach it by using dialogue.

Second is the *movement objective* or the *body objective*.

The body objective can be direct or indirect, conscious or subconscious.

Whether the body objective is direct or indirect, conscious or subconscious, all body movement, or *body phrasing*, is used to fill the important functions of enriching characterizations. These exercises will prepare you to do that.

In normal everyday life, when you stop for directions, it's only natural when the person points and says, "Go two blocks down," he is using a direct or conscious movement objective.

Let there be no possibility of misunderstanding. By movement I mean any small action of any part of your body. If you move your finger to the top of the page and then take hold of the page, you have used two units of motion. Then if you turn the page, you have used three, and so forth.

Exercise

While seated comfortably on your posture hook hold a book in your lap, but don't do anything with the book until after you start speaking the line of any speech, with enough pauses to carry you, in single units of motion—to an indirect body objective. This body objective is to locate and point to the last word on page 125 of the book.

During the reading of your speech, fill each pause with a single unit of motion. Make only one clean movement in one direction during each pause.

Doing these exercises are evidence of not cutting any corners, but paying the price to achieve naturalness. This kind of developed naturalness is the type that virtually every great performer possesses.

After you have gone through this experience, try other *action objectives*, while doing the "Quality of Mercy" speech. For example: peel a potato, dust furniture, or take clothing from a drawer any-thing—as your indirect body objective.

Make each unit head toward your objective.

Any movement you make, with *any* part of your body is a unit of motion. Each unit must be directed toward an *ultimate objective*.

Intention —what you want to accomplish immediately

Objective —what you want to accomplish *next*.

Goal —what you want to accomplish in the long run.

By taking its precise place in a chain of action, each unit becomes related to the ultimate objective.

This is what Stanislavski meant by units and objectives. A student of mine is so expert at this drill he can do the "Quality of Mercy" exercise with such precision and detailed control, that he can saddle his horse from start to finish, while going through the exercise.

Alternately practice the contemporary play speech and the "Quality of Mercy" speech. Make a consecutive series of natural, single units of motion in each pause. Make them lead toward a natural indirect, subconscious body objective. This will point you toward the habit of synchronizing natural actions and give you the correct start with any speech, using the First Law of Timing.

The First Law of Timing is a great *common denominator* and *connector* with real life.

The things you do while putting on your make-up, getting dressed, setting a table, driving a car, or working in the garden and so forth, all make good natural subconscious body objectives.

Remember whatever the action, an actor arrives at his movement objective by a series of units of motion.

As you learn to support your scenes with *consciously arrived*-at *subconscious* actions, built of units and objectives, you will grow into what is known as a natural actor. You will also be on your way toward acquiring the technique of timing.

CHAPTER TWELVE

The Second Law of Timing
(Move During The Phrase)

E very day on motion picture sound stages, in television studios, and the theater, you have opportunities and chances thrown at you. When you're cast in a production, you're given a final script, but this doesn't insure you against changes. During the actual production, scripts are constantly being revised. You may receive revisions at the last minute. Here your training and experience show through. You must wipe out what you've memorized and use the *Law of Substitution* quickly, accurately, and automatically.

You used your own pauses in the "Quality of Mercy" speech. Relearn the speech with these arbitrary pauses:

The quality of mercy is not strain'd, (*Pause*)
It droppeth as the gentle rain from heaven
Upon the place beneath: (*Pause*)
It is twice bless'd; (*Pause*)
It blesseth him that gives and him that takes: (*Pause*)
'Tis mightiest in the mightiest; (*Pause*)
It becomes the throned monarch better than his
     crown; (*Pause)*
His sceptre shows the force of temporal power,
     (*Pause*)
The attribute to awe and majesty, (*Pause*)
Wherein doth sit the dread and fear of kings; (*Pause*)
 But mercy is above this scepter'd sway, (*Pause*)
It is enthroned in the hearts of kings, (*Pause*)
It is an attribute to God himself, (*Pause*)
And earthly power doth then show likest God's
     (*Pause*)
When mercy seasons justice.

Another great common denominator with reality is the: *Second Law of Timing*—move during a spoken phrase.

Always start the movement with the first syllable of the first word and end the movement with the last sound of the last word.

Repeat the "Quality of Mercy" with the revised pauses, well memorized.

The first vocal phrase is "The quality of mercy is not strain'd."

The first syllable you hear in that phrase, is "thuh." The last syllable you hear is "ain'd."

Touch your knee with your fingers at the same time you say "thuh." Now touch your shoulder with the same fingers saying "ain'd."

Do this several times.

Fill in the remaining sounds and read the whole phrase. "The quality of mercy is not strain'd," touching your knee on "thuh" and your shoulder on "ain'd." Let your hand remain on your shoulder.

The second phrase is "It droppeth as the gentle rain from heaven upon the place beneath." Let your hand leave your shoulder on the sound of "ih," in the word "it" and touch your knee precisely on the "eath" sound, in the "beneath." Your hand remains on your knee.

The third phrase is "It is twice bless'd." Start your hand up on the "ih" sound in the word "it" to reach your shoulder exactly on the "est" sound in the word "bless'd." Your hand remains on your shoulder.

Obey the second Law of Timing, continue your knee-to shoulder and shoulder-to-knee action, in sequence, throughout the vocal phrases only of your "Quality of Mercy"

You've just used the laws of *ratio* and *proportion* that you learned in school. They'll keep your reading of the speech from becoming visually monotonous.

Here's why and how:

The number of words in our arbitrary vocal phrases varies considerably. But in this particular exercise, the same distance must be traveled by the physical action during each vocal phrase.

Therefore, either the physical action must be speeded up (or slowed down) to accommodate the length of the vocal phrase, or the speed of the vocal phrases must be dramatically changed to accommodate the actions.

In this case it is much better, as you can see—and hear—to accommodate the speed of the physical action to the length of the vocal phrase.

Going back to the beginning of the "Quality of Mercy" instead of using the knee-to-shoulder and shoulder-to-knee action during the vocal phrases, substitute our units of motion (eyes—head—smile—hands) using only one unit to each phrase. Next substitute any contemporary play speech for the "Quality of Mercy" using our arbitrary units of motion.

Now, still adhering strictly to the *second Law of Timing*, go through the "Quality of Mercy" speech, using a natural subconscious body objective, such as taking off your jacket.

Then for the "Quality of Mercy," substitute any modern play speech, using a natural, subconscious body objective.

You may have heard that some people are born with a sense of timing. If God has blessed you in this way—fine. If not—a sense of timing *can* be acquired.

Practice these exercises on the two laws of timing until you have perfect synchronization of movement and speech.

Never underestimate the power of the pause. It gives you a chance to do nothing, with sustained energy. Many a great comedian has made a career of pausing with sustained energy. The public loves these pauses as much as his lines.

So far your pauses have been logical.

Now, try the *psychological Pause.*

The psychological pause interrupts a body phrase or a vocal phrase. By starting a body phrase and interrupting, or stopping its action, while you insert a vocal phrase, you produce suspended motion.

By starting a vocal phrase and interrupting, or stopping the speech, while you insert a body phrase, you produce suspended sound. In both cases, you momentarily dam-up time. You create suspense!

Many working actors in film, television and theater use the psychological pause every day. It's the actor's "cliffhanger." It creates suspense, stimulates interest, causes surprise, stirs the imagination of the audience, and vitalizes the actor with a quality of excitement.

The psychological pause is so potent, it must be used sparingly, with sound motivation and good judgment. Otherwise it becomes too much of a good thing.

Learn to use your hands in meaningful ways, and avoid hiding them in the pockets. Baste pockets closed on costumes.

At one time or another, almost every actor stops short in a scene, flaps those things hanging on the ends of his arms and asks desperately, "What shall I do with my hands?"

You'll never have to go through that crisis. Timing body phrases into units and objectives—has given you the answer.

Now, your sense of timing is substituting habit patterns, constructed in the conscious mind, for relaxed habits in the subconscious.

CHAPTER THIRTEEN

Coordination
(Put It All Together)

To blend and mix action and speech takes *coordination*. *Coordination* is a beautiful thing to see and experience. Coordination is form in rhythmic motion.

We are going to simultaneously coordinate three units of motion into one multiple unit of motion—a body phrase, in which each individual part begins and ends at precisely the same instant.

Sit comfortably, hands on knees.

Exercise
Eyes right—hold it
Smile up—hold it
Left hand to top shirt button—hold it
 (Hold all three positions with energy.)

Simultaneously, move to:
Eyes center
Smile down
Hand on knee

Start all three units of motion at the same time and end them at the same time, regardless of the different distances each unit has to travel

The longest unit governs the various speeds of all the units. The hand has to travel further and faster than the eyes and the smile, in order to reach its objective and the same split second as the eyes and smile.

You have just used the laws of *ratio* and *proportion* to combine, simultaneously three units of motion into one coordinated unit of motion. By combining three units, under a controlled law you have made a new unit. You have experienced coordination.

Coordination Exercise

Create your own continuity cavalcade

Made up of these three-way units of motions.

(Sample)

1. Eyes right Right hand to the top shirt button Smile up

2. Eyes center Smile down Right hand down

3. Eyes right oblique down Smile up Right hand to top shirt button

Construct many similar coordinated three-way units of motion and practice them according to the following "formula."

Formula For Coordination Exercise

1. "Quality of Mercy"—First Law of Timing
2. Contemporary Scene—First Law of Timing
3. "Quality of Mercy"—Second Law of Timing
4. Modern Play Scene—Second Law of Timing

Use this formula with the following exercises leading toward controlled freedom.

An actor needs freedom to grow, expand, and develop according to his needs. However, when the desire for freedom has no "blueprint" or chart to follow, power is dissipated and impact lost.

Without organized freedom, the subconscious cannot create.

Undirected freedom causes the performance and the career to suffer. Uncontrolled freedom is a violation of basic principles.

To move on toward a balanced habit of controlled freedom, use the coordination formula and apply some full body action to it. This means using the entire body in free form or *abstract motions*.

Feel free to go into any wild pose you can take and hold.

Make sure that every bit of motion of the entire body—begins at the same moment, as though an electric current had been switched on. Make *equally* sure that every bit of motion ends at exactly the same instant, as though the current had been switched off. It is important in this exercise that there is absolutely no drag or drift—not the slightest extra movement of an eye, hand or foot, and so forth.

Make these abstract movements with energy and hold them with energy. Use relaxed constriction to hold them with energy. Holding the vitality at the ends of these movements helps develop a continuous line of energy.

The last of these coordination exercises has to do with the everyday work of an actor. The application of consciously organized form to a subconscious objective of a character.

Select a play speech. Search the speech carefully for any word—or words—that will give you a clue to consciously invent and develop a definite subconscious objective. Head toward this subconscious objective, one unit at a time, by applying the First Law of Timing, the second Law of Timing, or both laws of timing, as needed for interpretation.

If you don't find sufficient clues for a subconscious objective in the text of the speech, create them from the storehouse of your imagination such as playing a game of solitaire, writing a note, peeling an apple, or even looking up a number in the telephone book.

To develop dexterity and a fluidity of form in rhythmic motions, create and use many subconscious objectives to each speech you select to work on.

You are now aware of another great common denominator for acting and reality. How to use units and objectives as controls in the two laws of timing.

As you view motion pictures and television films (not the episodic or sit-com type that are found on television) notice the actors are usually holding something or doing something that has nothing at all to do with the actual dialogue. But it has *everything* to do with naturalness. It is a beautiful thing to see, but unfortunately hard to find in a lot of television and motion pictures these days. This is because of lack of time for preparation, poor training, or lack of desire by the actors to be truly professional.

My sincere desire and the reason for this book is to impart my knowledge in the hope that such poor acting, especially in today's television, will dramatically improve.

I can be sure of this: The information is available again and I feel I've done my best in presenting it. My prayer is that you will take this information to heart and become such skilled craftsmen, that the public will demand nothing less.

CHAPTER FOURTEEN

Imagination
(A Background Of Findings)

E very action meets with a reaction. This ultimately leads to opposition of purposes, which is good because we need all the problems to solve that grow out of this. This activity is the basis of dramatic conflict and our art.

It is your job as an actor to understand the objectives and the reverse objectives as well, so that you can interweave a character's personality with your own. You must be so intimate with the character that you can consciously supply it with its own subconscious.

In order to attain this relationship, a conscious, subconscious technique is a must for the actor.

We must have the gift to identify ourselves with other persons, to relive their experience and to feel its conflicts as our own....in order that we shall feel in their lives what we know in our own; the human dilemma."

—*J. Bronowski*

If in real life, you are told a few things about a complete stranger whom you are going to meet—

If you meet that stranger and hear him speak a few hundred words—

If you overhear a few people say a few hundred words about him—

You have a very meager introduction. I doubt if you could consider this person a close acquaintance, they would not be considered a close personal friend, and you certainly would not consider this person as your second self.

Yet, this is exactly what actors are expected to do.

An actor must take a few words, written by the writer, describing the character he will play—

Take a few hundred words said by the character—

Take a few hundred words said to the character by other characters in the play—

Take a few hundred words of explanation and interpretation by a director and—

From this meager introduction, an actor must develop a relationship, that is intimate enough to create audience identification with the character he is portraying.

The imagination allows the actor to empathize

with the character or to feel with the character. The actor must learn to adopt the dialogue as his own. Through empathy, this is accomplished. The act and character are now one.

An actor is the alchemist who is expected to take all the elements and put them together and produce an illusion that is spellbinding to an audience. Once again, his first priority is the believability and truthfulness of the character. Each actor eventually develops his own way of accomplishing this, but the basic know-how is the same and the end result must be the same: *audience identification.*

To develop this relationship between the actor and the character, the actor must use every common denominator between real life and acting that he can possibly learn.

We have discussed at length one of these common denominators: *The two laws of timing,* which organize speech and action.

We will now use a second: *The Law of Substitution*—to consciously construct a subconscious for the character.

By using the Law of Substitution, the actor can substitute the character's personality for his own while interjecting his own personality to flavor the character he is portraying. I'll list some scenes from a motion picture script, including a "description" of the central character by the author and some "direction" by the director.

You'll obtain:

1. A few words of description by the writer

2. A few words of description by the director

3. A few words spoken by the central character

4. A few words said by the central character

5. A few words said about the central character by two different people.

From this information, you must pick enough "clues" to thoroughly know your central character, his personality traits, characteristics, inhibitions, fears, environment, social background—every clue you can find pertaining to the central character *Mackey*, and his situation. From these you will give *Mackey* a subconscious of his own.

(Memorize Mackey's Speech)

FADE IN

I-INT. CELL—NIGHT—MED.

On Earl Mackey, a slender red-headed man with clear gray eyes and slow, lumbering movements. He is sitting on a bunk. On a small table in front of him we see the trial transcripts and newspaper scrapbook from which the context of this picture was taken.

(Director's Note) Mackey must play this scene with numbness. It must be with the feeling of a man that has completely given up.

MACKEY

My name is Earl Mackey. Three times I have died. Most people will only die once. Sudden death is easy. But, when you know the week, the day and the hour that you are going to die.... You die a little with each second. When they pull the switch, you're already dead.

(Pause)

I have died three times.... Three times I have gone through the last twenty-four hours of my life.

10—CLOSE SHOT—JACOBS   10

JACOBS

Little Frankie was my little girl, and now she's dead.... She didn't know who it was. She just said "An old redheaded man, Daddy." That's all my little girl could say.

DISSOLVE TO:

11—CLOSE SHOT—MRS. COOK   11

MRS. COOK

Why, Earl Mackey lived with us for just about two years. Why, he could take care of my little girl just as well as I could, and if he was free today he could come right back here. I'd still trust him with my children.

20—INT. COURTROOM—DAY—CLOSE SHOT OF RUTH, FRANKIE'S SISTER, ON WITNESS STAND.   20

RUTH

Yes, Sir. We asked her, "Who did that?" And she said, "The red-headed man at the boathouse."

75—MEDIUM SHOT—DEFENSE ATTORNEY ANDREWS   75

ANDREWS

There's still a lot of difference between "An" and "The." There just might be enough difference to save a man's life.... At least to get another reprieve.

After you have listed the clues, compare them with the following sample clues:

Clues from playwright:
  Death cell
  Slender
  Red-headed
  Gray eyes
  Clear eyes
  Slow—lumbering

Clues from Director:
  Numbness
  Given Up Hope
  Faced death three times
  In a position where he's had to think of it over a set period of time

Clues from one person talking which indicates some background of incident:
  A little girl is dead
  She lived a little while after the incident which brought on her death
  She didn't know who brought on the incident
  She knew it was an *"old"* man
  She knew it was "a red-headed man"

Clues from woman who knew Mackey:
  Lived in household
  Lived there two years

Took care of little girl as well as mother could
If he was free, he could come back
The mother trusts him completely with her children

Clues from victim's sister on witness stand:
Victim lived for a while after the incident that brought on her death
Only made one statement
"The" man "Red-headed" man
From boathouse

Clues from defense attorney:
Conflict between "an" and "the"
Save a man's life
Another reprieve

Focus your "aware beam" on the clues and the conflicting clues and from your imagination develop an image of the character.

Focus your "aware beam" on this image until Mackey becomes vividly clear. Use the clues and your imagination as material and tools to construct—consciously *Mackey*'s subconscious personality, personality mannerisms, traits, and so forth. By using the Law of Substitution, move your own personality aside as far as you can and function with awareness within *Mackey*'s personality.

Answer the following questions as if you were *Mackey*:

What is you name? (Answer *Earl Mackey*)

How old are you?:

Where were you born?

What nationality were your mother and father?

Do you remember the house you lived in?

How long did you live there?

What was it like?

Describe in detail the house and each room, particularly your own room (as you remember).

What did your father do for a living?

Did you mother work?

Were there any brothers or sisters?

What is you first memory?

Where and when did you start school?

Make up more questions and give the answers.

From your storehouse of imagination, recall every possible detail that can help you develop your "Mackey's personality.

These questions and answers consciously put you into Mackey's not-so-imaginary subconscious life.

You can't give *Mackey* a full psychoanalysis, but you can develop a *background of findings*, which will serve your purposes as an actor.

Develop your background to the point of the memorized dialogue with a consciously constructed subconscious.

Don't try to act the speech. Let it be the outgrowth of this background you've put into *Mackey's* "if" life.

What you are able to do now is the result of a steady progression which started with your "aware beam" focused on a hand signal in the pauses of the "Quality of Mercy" excerpt and flooded with life by the imagination from your subconscious.

By breaking the life of *Mackey* down into its finest parts (lowest common denominators), you will find that it will reassemble itself into a complete whole with a solid line made up of small units.

In building a part, if you have trouble at any particular scene, go back to the segment that motivated that scene and break it down to still finer details in your imagination.

Because you have had faith and kept yourself aware, you have reached an understanding of how to use the actor's *laws of timing* and the *laws of substitution*.

These laws are mathematically true.
They are scientifically true.
They are logically true.
They are artistically true.

You have created and transmitted emotion by your craftsman's use of tools you forged mechanically.

You are beginning to master the science underlying the art of acting. You also understand how impossible it would be to improve upon God's natural creative process. You're learning how to live in harmony *with* this process, and that is truly awe inspiring.

CHAPTER FIFTEEN

Emotional Flexibility
(Creative Expression)

In this chapter, you'll be forging a key that will open one of the most important doors to the art of acting!

You will be given a series of emotional flexibility and control exercises. When you first practice these exercises, gradually step by step you will be able to go further and further into each emotion.

After practicing the emotional exercises for several days, you will grow aware of each emotion and how it produces a definite delineation. You will see each one standing clean, clear, and completely definable, despite any similarity of muscular action in the exercises. In a short time, you'll be aware that your muscular reactions are as varied as the emotions that stimulate them.

Once again your subconscious is a vast natural reservoir of creativity, inspiration and emotional power.

Imagination releases the creativeness and emotional power of that reservoir.

If you were standing at the bottom of an empty swimming pool and I started to fill the pool with water, you could first feel it with your feet, then your ankles, then your calves, your knees, thighs, stomach, chest, neck, mouth, and nose, until the water finally reached your eyes.

Use this imagination formula for the following series of exercises.

While doing these exercises, let your body respond naturally to your imagination. Don't try to force yourself into a particular physical mold. Let any mold and movement be the result of your thoughts—no superimposed attitudes, ideas, or gestures. I'm not telling you "what to do," but "to do" what you might imagine under these selected sets of circumstances.

While performing these emotional scales, carefully note and be aware of how they affect your heartbeat and the rhythm of your breathing.

After every exercise, take a few steps around the room to clear your head.

Emotional Flexibility Exercises
First Exercise—**Anger**

Concentrate deeply and imagine you are angry. You have never been so angry in your life.... Let this feeling of anger travel slowly up your body. Feel it first with your feet.... When you are angry your feet will grip the floor.... Then feel the anger travel up your ankles...your calves...legs.... Your knees will flex as you get set to give or take a blow.... Anger travels on up your thighs...your stomach...your chest...pouring out through your arms to your hands, which will probably become fists or claws.... On goes the anger, up through your neck to your lips, which will very likely become thin and taut.... Finally it reaches your eyes, where your audience looks straight into your imagined feelings.

Slowly come out of this exercise by drawing the anger from your "self" beginning with your eyes and ending with your toes until your body is at ease once again.

Second Exercise-Sadness

You are very sad...you have never been so sad in your life. Your feet are heavy and tired. Your ankles are sore and swollen. Your knees are so weak, they will hardly support the weight of your body...even your stomach is sick and there is a dark, heavy feeling in and around you. Your heart is hurting and about to break. Your breath is labored. Your hands are so heavy, your arms can hardly carry their weight. Your throat is dry and sore...you can't swallow and your lips are dry. Your eyes are tired and bloodshot. Let all the strength drain out of you into the earth, until you can hardly move at all.

When you have gone as far as you can without breaking into a sob, *slowly*, ever so slowly, come out of the exercise.

Third Exercise—Pride

You are very proud. You have never been so tall and proud in all your life. Your feet are firm on the earth. Your legs are straight and lithe. Your hips are taut and slender. Your chest is high and buoyant. Your face is bright and shinning Your eyes are clear and clean. The wind blows through your hair, and as you stand there in your great pride gradually, very slowly, come out of the exercise.

Fourth Exercise—Fear

You are frightened. More frightened than you have ever been before in all your life. You may be killed in a few moments. Your feet want to run, but they can't because they're so heavy. Your knees are about to buckle. Your flesh creeps. Your entire being tries to hide within itself. Your voice sticks in your throat. At any moment you may be dead now.

When you have taken the exercise as far as you can, slowly come out of it.

Fifth Exercise—Happiness

You are happy. Your feet are eager and alert. Your legs almost dance with joy. Your chest is light and buoyant. You can almost float away. Your smile is happy. Your eyes sparkle and your face shines.

Carry the exercise as far as you can; then ever so slowly, come out of it.

As you practice these exercises, you'll go further and further into each emotion. You will confirm how far you can delve into each one and still retain dependable control of yourself and your technique.

In time, your sensitivity and control will increase and you will see each delineation becoming cleaner, clearer, and more defined.

Return to each of the emotional flexibility and control exercises; this time when you reach the very top of each emotion—right at the peak—speak a line of dialogue. Whatever the emotion you're working on, it's best to use a very short line with it.

For example, in the emotion of anger, use the line "I'll hit you!" Or, the emotion of pride, use the line, "That's my dad!"

I must warn you, don't think of how you're going to say the line, or how it should sound. Let your interpretation of the line be entirely the result of your controlled emotion. It will be difficult at first. Eventually, you will be able to speak the line spontaneously, allowing the emotion itself to give the words their interpretation.

You will develop daring. You won't care how the line sounds, so long as it has controlled emotion behind it.

You are ready now for your next exercise. This is the transference from one emotion to another. It's called *emotional transition*.

Exercise
(Emotional Transition)

Using the emotion of fear, build it up as high as you can go. When you reach the top, instead of slowly coming out of it, as you previously did, transfer it to the high peak of your happiness emotion. *Slowly* come out of the exercise.

As you keep on working on the exercise, you will begin to perform the *emotional transition* with the ease and skill of a professional. Try various series of transitions, using all the emotions and situations in the preceding exercises. You will also want to invent some of your own: jealously, haughtiness, greed, and so forth.

These variations will give you a greater range of flexibility. Your emotional scale will be broad and controlled because of your hard work.

This is going to provide you with a substantial set of emotional tools, which you can count on whenever you need them. These exercises will in short give you controlled emotional flexibility.

CHAPTER SIXTEEN

Relaxation
(Autogenic and Progressive)

> *The mind is it's own place, and in itself can make a Heaven of Hell or Hell of Heaven.*
>
> *—John Milton*

The dictionary says to relax is to be less tight, severe or strict. As you will see in a future chapter dealing with the voice, a tight throat restricts the air flow necessary for the full rich voice you need as an actor.

Stress and *tension* not only affect the voice adversely but also the body and mind. So they *affect the whole actor.*

With the fast paced business of motion pictures, television and theater, tension is just another aspect of the business, just like props or scenery. The trick is to learn how to deal with it or how to use it, instead of it using you.

Relaxation is so important that another whole book could and should be written about it just for actors. Relaxation is the *key* to becoming a natural actor. For without it, you cannot hope to characterize creatively, think on your feet, or react correctly. It stifles or restricts *every one* of the actor's tools you've made for yourself. It severely limits any technique that is useful to the actor.

Relaxation, as with emotional flexibility, is a learned skill, and it's locked in place with repetition and practice. You will become so proficient at relaxation, you'll be able to turn it on just like a light. Once you have mastered this chapter you will have discovered one of the most important keys to acting!

The key (technique) is much the same as the emotional flexibility scale of the last chapter. As you felt the emotion with your feet, ankles, legs, waist, hips, torso, and so forth, so will you learn to relax *progressively* as well as *autogenically*.

For these two exercises you will need to get very comfortable, either in a recliner or lying down on a sofa or where you can relax your entire body. Wear non-restrictive clothing and take your shoes off.

You may record the exercises or memorize them (which may take a while.) They must, however, be repeated word for word. Most of my students can memorize two pages of dialogue in about thirty minutes. It may take you longer at first, don't worry about it. You are about to do something very important right now. Learn how to relax!

Exercise
(Autogenic Relaxation)

Begin to breathe in slowly and easily. You will relax quickly just breathing slowly and easily.

Now, let your eyes close. As you do so say to yourself, "I feel myself relaxing. All of the muscular tension is draining out of me." Begin sinking into the chair. Begin thinking about allowing your body to relax deeply.

Put your head in a comfortable position; let it lie back. Your neck muscles relax and your shoulders droop. Your back sinks and your arms are heavy at your side.

The pelvic area relaxes and your legs and feet begin to feel heavy, and you begin to drift back into a very comfortable state of relaxation and ease.

Now, relax yourself inside. Starting with your head, say to yourself, "My scalp and brain are loose and relaxed; my eyes, nose, mouth, jaw and throat muscles are relaxed. My esophagus and all my vital organs are relaxed and tranquil, as are my chest, back, stomach, hips, legs and feet. My insides are totally relaxed and calm."

As you relax even further, your body will let go completely and you will drift back very comfortably. Letting go more and more, the further back you go, deeply relaxing.

You flow so comfortably inside as you begin to relax and let go.

The things in the world around you begin to fade further and further into the background, just as your cares and concerns begin to fade. The noises and distractions around you fade becoming less and less important. They become almost unnoticeable as you drain inside.

Your muscles begin to feel very heavy. There's a limpness and looseness in your body. You feel so totally and completely relaxed. Say to yourself, "I am totally relaxed."

You withdraw inside to your thoughts and fantasies as they flow quietly and comfortably.

You relax down and let go. You sink further and further back. Your body goes very deeply into a state of muscle relaxation. All of your vital functions slow down and become regular.

You relax deep. You feel so very relaxed, calm and peaceful.

You go even further now. A peaceful flowing— a peaceful deep sense of tranquillity—as with every breath you go further. As you breathe out, you feel the muscles let go just a little more. Perhaps your shoulders and neck relax a little more, or your stomach or legs, or feet. With every breath you sink a little further into deep relaxation.

Your conscious mind flows so comfortably now, so easily. Your subconscious begins to surface, to be more accessible. The subconscious becomes conditioned more and more to accept suggestions and thoughts. Your subconscious is opening wide in acceptance of the good suggestions you will be giving yourself to enhance your state of relaxation to achieve total control over stress and anxiety. (Now you state each stressful emotion or feeling whether imagined or real.)

Say to yourself "My anxieties about being able to memorize my lines are gone. My worries about a sloppy posture are gone because I will always stay in the V shape, with the help of relaxed constriction, and I will stay on my hook always," and so forth. List all of your anxieties and affirm that you have changed all bad habits into new good ones, with the help of the law of substitution. Give yourself good healthy suggestions to help your acting career and every phase of your life.

Now, as you relax very deeply, you will go even further back to the most tranquil and calm place you have ever experienced. It may be the beach at the ocean, the cool mountains with fluffy white cottony clouds, or it may be your own backyard. You may hear a bird sing or the waves come in. As you lie there you begin to sink into the chair and become a part of the place you are in, sinking more and more right into the earth. Going to the very deepest level of relaxation now, deep, deep slowing down—way down inside. Just as you will experience the sensation of tranquillity and peacefulness in the hours and days ahead, you will build your career, as your life, upon the solid foundation.

Your body will function without unnecessary stress. You will find that you are going to be very calm as you go about your daily studies and activities.

You are learning how to control your own anxieties and stress more and more every day.

As you become more free of stress, your mind will focus sharper and clearer on the tools you are building for your acting career. All of the good suggestions you will be giving yourself during these times of total relaxation will start to pay huge dividends.

You will quickly and easily absorb the fundamentals of acting and move on to advanced techniques. The more you relax and let go, the sooner you learn. Each exercise you breath in will expose itself to your conscious mind and then be pulled down into your subconscious. When this exercise is over you will be alert and feel rested and peaceful inside. All tensions and discomforts will be gone, and you will be relaxed and refreshed and stay that way. Each time you do this exercise you will be able to go further and further into relaxation and all the good healthy suggestions you will be giving yourself. (End of exercise.)

The way we talk to ourselves can lead to stressful emotions. Our thoughts and actions pretty well decide what will happen with us. Ask yourself, "How much can this thing I'm worried about really affect me except for the meaning I attach to it?" So remember our perceptions largely create stress.

Now just relax and breathe deep. Get up and walk around a bit before the next exercise. You may not remember all of the exercise just now, but it doesn't bother you. Matter of fact, nothing does.

As you prepare for the next exercise in much the same way you did the last one, make your goal of relaxation more than just the words. Breathe it into your very being with every breath. Focus your mental attention on the various muscles indicated as the exercise progresses. Let your breathing remain calm and regular even when tensing a muscle group. Oxygen helps the relaxation to occur. Do not hold your breath.

Exercise
(Progressive Relaxation)

Begin by focusing your attention on your dominant hand. Lift your hand at the wrist and make a fist. Hold the tension for about five seconds, then tighten it more. Take a deep breath and let go of all the tension as you exhale, saying to yourself "Relax."

Now concentrate your attention on your other hand. Lift it at the wrist and make a fist. Hold the tension for about five seconds, then tighten it still tighter. Take a deep breath and slowly let all the tension go, as you slowly exhale the breath, saying to yourself "Relax."

Focus your attention on your dominant arm, holding it up at the elbow, tense the big muscle, elbow, forearm, and wrist and hand. Hold the tension about one-two-three-four and five, then tense a little more, take a deep breath and exhale as you let the tension go, saying to yourself "Relax," as you return your arm to your side.

Now do the other arm the same way. Now do both legs the same way. Concentrate your attention on your shoulders. Tighten your shoulders by bringing your head down between them as far as you can. Shrug your shoulders for about five seconds. Make the shrug a little tighter as you take a deep breath, exhale and let the tension go at the same time you say to yourself "Relax." Notice the feeling of warmth as you say the word "Relax" again.

Lift your dominant hand at the wrist again with less tension this time count to five and relax your hand. Notice the difference between this lesser tension and the relaxation.

Do your other hand the same way.

By progressively using less tension you have now observed the cumulative effect of this relaxation technique.

As you continue throughout your whole body, remember to breathe easily.

Take a slow deep breath between each part of the tension releasing exercise. Notice the pleasant warmth. Now concentrate on breathing as you exhale say to yourself, "Relax" and "Breathe normally."

One more time—take a slow, deep breath. Let it out slowly, saying to yourself, "Relaxed, heavy, warm."

Now close your eyes tightly and count to five and relax. Arch your eyebrows up and count to five. Relax. Now concentrate on the muscles of your forehead and tighten them—count to five and say to yourself "Relax." Now concentrate on the muscles in the center of your face. Scowl and wrinkle your nose. Hold it for a five count with tension, then drain the energy. Next widen out your cheeks and brows. Count to five and relax yourself. Purse your lips—count to five and relax. Smile broadly to five and relax. Now drop your jaw, relaxing the muscles of your tongue and throat. Count to five and say to yourself "Relax."

Take a deep breath and exhale slowly. Notice the feeling. Enjoy the feeling of total relaxation.

Notice the way your body feels, warm and flowing easily.

Lie still for five minutes in your fantasy land before returning to your daily activities. (End of exercise.)

Within a week you will begin to see the results of these relaxation exercises. Great results. God made our bodies to function in a relaxed state, not under bright lights, loud noises and extreme conditions, but now you know the secret of staying *relaxed all the time*, whether under these situations or calm ones. After thorough daily practice you won't even have to lie down or close your eyes to do the exercise. You're doing a natural thing when you relax and once again nature is on your side. Get these exercises down before going to the next chapter as they will prepare you for dealing with your subconscious.

> *Men are not worried by things, but by their ideas about things. When we meet with difficulties or become anxious and troubled, let us not blame others but ourselves, that is, our ideas about things.*
> —*Epictetus*

Relaxation Techniques for Directors and Students
(*Presented by Mary Ann Fletcher —Director of Theater*)

Please note — Many of the following techniques have been borrowed from other sources ... while others are originals.

Exercises to do anytime ... Anywhere

Controlled Deep Breathing —Purpose: to get more oxygen to the brain.

Slowly inhale for 5 seconds, hold for 5 seconds, slowly exhale for 5 seconds.

Slowly inhale for 10 seconds, hold for 110 seconds, slowly exhale for 10 seconds.

Increase the time, as much as possible, to reach maximum amount of oxygen. It is best to be seated as some people get dizzy.

Temporary Transfer of Tension —Purpose: transfers tension to focused point on demand. This exercise is especially helpful to control shaky hands.

Grip, as tightly as possible, a solid object for a few seconds; then relax. Repeat until muscles relax. I lips quiver, press together tightly; then relax. Repeat quivering subsides.

Exercises to Do as a Group ... or Alone

For the neck—Purpose: helps relieve tension in the neck area.

Press the head as far right as possible towards the right shoulder. Don't raise the shoulder. Rotate the head down to the chest, then to the left shoulder. Then raise the head straight up and over to the right shoulder again. Avoid rotating the head back. Repeat several times. then reverse.

For the shoulders—Purpose: helps relieve tension in the shoulders & upper back.

Rotate the shoulders as far up, forwards, down, and back as possible. Repeat and reverse.

1. With legs slightly apart, lean as far to the right as possible, then forward & down, to the left, and to the back. Repeat several times, then reverse.

2. Lie on the floor, on the back, with arms to the side & legs extended in a straight line with the body. Lift the right leg straight up. Slowly cross it over the body & touch the floor with the right foot. Lift the leg straight up again, then slowly back to its original position. Repeat with the left leg, crossing body, etc. Keep the shoulders on the floor.

3. Push the imaginary wall by leaning as far forward as possible & stretching palms as far in front as possible, with hands pushing imaginary wall. "Shake it out" after exercise to relax muscles.

For the legs—Purpose: teaches how to relax muscles in the legs on command. Sit on the floor with legs extended out it front. Pull feet up, flex all leg muscles. relax. Repeat.

For the entire body—Purpose: to teach the entire body to relax on command. Especially helpful just prior to a performance or when trying to go to sleep. Soft music often helps intensify exercise. Mats can be used.

1. Lie on the floor, with lights dim or out, on your back. arms to the side, & legs relatively close together. Remove your shoes. If in a group, make sure everyone has their own space with no one touching anyone else. Do not cross your feet. Beginning with the top of your head, tense every muscle possible in the head. face,

etc. Spread tension down neck, into shoulders, down arms, into hands & fingers, down torso, upper thigh, knees, calves, ankles, feet, toes until entire body is tense. Then in reverse order. drain tension from toes. feet, ankles, etc. working all the way back up to the top c f the head until the tension has been released & the entire body drained of energy. Repeat several times. Make sure everyone has their own space & eyes are closed. If this is performed in class, notify office not to disturb you.

2. Go to your imaginary haven. (Mine is the beach.) Close your eyes & imagine yourself on a warm & sandy beach. Go for a walk, feeling the warm sand between your toes, the soothing breeze, and the warm sun. Walk to the water's edge & feel the tide come in over your toes. Watch the waves come in & go back out. Listen to the surf. Hear the sea gulls & the ship's low distant horn. Walk slowly along the beach, feeling the water on your feet, the sun on your face. After awhile, turn around and feel the sun on your back. Walk slowly back, along the surf's edge, until you return to where you were. Slowly sit down. Imagine a soft blue light coming toward you. The closer it gets, the larger it gets until it finally encompasses you. After awhile. it slowly leaves you. You watch it float away until it becomes only a small dot, then finally disappears. The moment

it's gone, you hear your favorite song being played just for you. When your song is over. slowly open your eyes.

CHAPTER SEVENTEEN

Dialogues Dual-Track
(Spoken And Unspoken)

D ual track contains the audible sound track of dialogue and the silent track of thought. Both motivate reaction and help develop a fully rounded natural characterization.

Some actors dual-track instinctively. They do it to a greater or lesser degree—with technical awareness, or in a hit and miss manner. Great performers dual-track all the time—in every rehearsal and in every performance.

Reacting is as important to a scene as acting. Sometimes it is *more* important. Dual-tracking is the reactor of acting. It controls the spoken dialogue. It constructs a solid continuous line of concentration, developed from the actor's creative imagination as a substructure to support the words he speaks.

We borrow the phrase dual-track from motion picture terminology. In making a motion picture film the speech can be recorded on one track and the score (music) and sound effects in unison on another. These two tracks are run simultaneously and blended into a single unified track. This is mechanical double-track. The actor must use mental double-track.

With every line of dialogue, there must be a line of thought. Created from the actor's imagination and memorized word for word just as the line of dialogue.

The reaction of a person on the receiving end of a line of dialogue is as important and significant to a play (and its audience) as the spoken line itself.

Every actor must find out what goes into the art of reacting. He then must perfect the technique of reacting. The tool for this is *dual-track*. It is set in motion by the other actors' delivery and locked in place by listening.

Dual-track is an important function in the training of an actor's mind. It recognizes the existence of two trains of thought going on at the same time (in real life) in parallel lines to each other. It incorporates this realistic process into the technique of acting.

To repeat: Dual-track constructs a solid continuous line of concentration, developed from the actor's creative imagination, as a substructure to support the words he speaks. A line of concentration is the power line that transmits *empathy* from the actor to the audience. Without this, there is no empathy.

Without empathy, there is no "truth!"

Truth is the result of the substructure upon which the dialogue rides. The substructure is the result of dual track.

Many times the director will call for more intensity (more reaction); many actors, especially newcomers, respond by mugging or making bigger gestures. This isn't what he wants. He wants and needs more thought process. There has to be a reason for your reaction. If the thought is there, it will show through, in reaction. There is a natural responsive rhythm between action and reaction. Perfect timing takes place by following that rhythm.

When you dual-track in a role, you're doing a natural thing. You are completing a rhythmic pattern and giving your senses the benefit of faultless timing. In both the conscious objective of a role and the subconscious objective of its dual-track, you obey the laws of timing.

You have become aware of three of the actor's great common denominators now. *Timing and substitution form the sides of a triangle. Substitution on one side. timing on the other. At the apex of the triangle is dual-track. It is the peak achievement* that results from the substitution timing support.

Everything that is in substitution is in dual-track. Everything that is in timing is in dual-track. *It is this ultimate common denominator*. It contains all the other common denominators. It elevates the craft to the art of acting.

At this peak, all parts are reduced to their lowest common denominator of real life, where they come from in the first place and reassemble to create a whole person of consciously assumed reality.

The following scenes will show you how to dual-track, when working with another actor, listen to his lines for dual-track clues. In performance, dual-track is a combination of the audible soundtrack and a silent track of *connected mind pictures*.

In training, it is more effective at first to dual track aloud—memorizing the exact words that come from your imagination. Then, silently, think these words exactly as you memorize them. Later this silent dual-track will be transmitted from thought into instantaneous mind pictures.

When you translate this thought line into a series of connected mind pictures, your acting will begin to have that exciting, vital quality for which every good actor strives.

Your dual-track image for the following scenes will be different from mine. Your interpretation of the character's inner thoughts will not be the same as mine. The important thing is to keep the interpretation honest and within the framework of the characters as you understand them.

The silent dual-track you invent must be thought and rethought just as conscientiously as the audible part of the scene is learned (memorized). Only then will it become an automatic habit-pattern that will be dependable under the tensions of actual performance and help you keep up with the speed of modern film making.

In the following scenes, the parenthetical italicized lines are some of the possible dual-track thoughts and reactions. When a thought becomes a mind picture, it takes only a fraction of a second to flash its message. After all the whole process by which thought is translated into speech is still a mystery. We only know that it happens. It happens so quickly that literally before I know what I am thinking I already have said it. In the following scene *Ruth* can speculate about *the man* at the registration desk and size him up in the brief moment it takes her to say, *"Yeah?"*

Exercise Scene #1

The lobby of a shabby, third-rate hotel. Tom, *a personable young man, enters. He looks around for a moment, then walks over to the registration desk and taps the bell. In a few seconds* Ruth, *a flashy young girl, enters from a door behind the desk, taking up her place at the desk.*

RUTH

(*Who's this guy? He's not the kind who stays in a hotel* like this.)

Yeah?

(*Not bad lookin'. Probably up to somethin.'*)

What do you want?

TOM

(*Hm-m quite a dish for a flea bag like this. I wonder if she's Ruth?*)

Fix me up with a room?

RUTH

(*Looks like he's got some dough.*)

What do you want, double or single?

TOM

(*Well they told me to get acquainted with her regardless of what it costs.*)

Maybe you'd better fix me up with a double-just in case.

(*Boy that's a corny line. I must be slipping.*)

RUTH

(*Fresh guy but kinda cute.*)

Do you want a bath or not?

TOM

(*Here I go again.*)

Well, I've had one but I could probably stand another.

(That one really stinks. too. It must be the atmosphere around here.)

RUTH

(Same price. kid even if you are cute.)

Number six. That'll be two dollars.

TOM

(What a dive! Anything for the job though.)

Two dollars? Here it is. Cheap at half the price.

RUTH

(Cheap huh? Who does he think he is!)

That's a good room.

TOM

(I've got to get this in writing for the record.)

Do you want me to sign anything?

RUTH

(Gee he's got me running around in circles.)

Oh, yeah. You've got to register.

TOM

(Here's a chance to find out if this is Ruth.

Maybe I can trick her into telling me.)

(*As he writes out his name, he spells it.*)

   T-o-m R-o-g-e-r-s

   What's yours?

RUTH

(*Taken by surprise but not for long.*)

   Ruth Jac—

(*For the luva—Man! He's a fast one.*)

   Doesn't make any difference what
   mine is.

TOM

(*Better watch my step.*)

   You're right.

(*Flattery can't hurt. Anyhow its the truth.*)

   With a shape like yours, it doesn't
   make any difference what you name
   is.

RUTH

(*He's sharp. Notices everything.*)

   You know all the answers, don't you?

TOM

(*She's not sore. Think she really likes this corn-ball line.*)

Sure. I worked my way through college—selling a book—What Every Young Girl Should Know.

RUTH

(*I can keep up with you, fella.*)

Yeah, I know—I wrote it.

(*Let's get back to business. I don't want him to think I'm too anxious.*)

Do you want to go to your room now?

TOM

(*Ugh can hardly face the thought.*)

Well, I want to, but I've got some business in town.

(*Little more of the old pitch now.*)

You have things all comfy for me when I come back, will you?

RUTH

(*Picking up his bag.*)

(*This guy's pretty sure of himself!*)

I'll do that. I'll raise the window and
turn on the hot water for you.

TOM

(She'll be a pushover I hope.)

So long, Dreamboat.

Exercise Scene No. 2

A lawyer's office. Johnson, *a simple, honest, hard-
working man, is attempting to explain to an attorney
how he was tricked into giving a criminal alibi, making
it possible for the real killer to go free and an innocent
man to be convicted.*

JOHNSON

*(Oh. Lord. how did I ever get into this! Will he
believe me? He's got to believe me!)*

I was a transient

(Better give it to him straight.)

and I had been drinking.

(So help me. it's the truth.)

I haven't heard anything about the
little girl.

(What a fool I was. I thought they were trying to find out about the fight. I'm afraid the law's not going to like this.)

So I didn't tell the sheriff anything except what time it was when I was drinking with Red.

(If I just hadn't let him trick me. If I'd just never met him.)

After I found out about

(The kid dead. dead!)

the little girl being killed,

(If I'd just been smarter!)

I knew Red had tricked me into alibiing for him.

(Just as well get it over with.)

Well, I was drinking with him one day,

(Yeah. it sure adds up now.)

And he seemed so anxious for me to remember what time it was.

(If he'll just believe me. It's the truth.)

Seemed a little nervous

(I shouldn't a got so loaded.)

122

but, he'd been drinking quite a lot of
wine.

*(If I'd just been sober. I'd have caught on. Well.
I didn't think much about it. at that time. How
could I know it was a thing like that?)*

I was kidding him about the scratches
on his face.

(Yes. he told me—and I believed it!)

He told me

(The liar. The dirty rotten. killing liar!)

he walked into a plum tree.

Exercise Scene No. 3

The lavish drawing room of Mrs. Maude Rayden, *a
wealthy society woman who has just returned from a
club meeting. She enters the room and see her daughter*
Joyce, *who is thumbing through a magazine.*

MAUDE

*(Mm-m—so there's my new Harper's Bazaar.
I'll tell her now.)*

Oh, Joyce, I'm so glad you're home.

(She'll love this. Simply love it!)

We've discovered the most
wonderful thing for the Junior
League to do this year while the
fleet's in town.

JOYCE

(I can just imagine!)

Have you—joined the Junior League,
Mother?

MAUDE

(What a flippant sense of humor young people
have today.)

No, dear, but I'll tell you what to do
and you can do it.

JOYCE

(You're always telling me what to do.)

But, Mother, I'm not the entire Junior
League. It might be that—

MAUDE

(She should have more self-confidence. After all.
she's my daughter.)

Nonsense, my dear. If you want the
League to have a party for all those
nice sailor boys, they'll just have it.
That's all there is to it.

124

JOYCE

*(How grim!)*Oh, do I want to have a party
for the—er—Navy?

MAUDE

(That's better. She just needs handling.)

Of course you do—don't you?

JOYCE

(Grim? This is positively revolting.)

Well, up to the present moment I
hadn't given it a great deal of
thought—in fact, it comes as a
complete surprise to me.

*(Mother's always so busy. Probably comes of
having nothing to do.)*

I suppose you and the other members
of your little sewing circle have been
sitting around a tea table at the
Fairmont all afternoon, planning
ways and means of keeping your
respective daughters out of trouble.

(They should talk!)

You want to watch out that some of
you older gals don't get into trouble
yourselves, Mother dear.

MAUDE

(Really! I wonder if she could have heard—of course not.)

Joyce, sometimes I don't quite understand you. That's what comes of letting you lead your own life, as you call it. None of you—not one of your set has any respect for her mother.

JOYCE

(That's right up on your soapbox.)

Oh, Mother, now let's not start that again.

(Might as well get this over.)

Now tell me what is this great plan of yours to entertain the Navy?

MAUDE

(There now. she's being more reasonable.)

We believe it would be nice if the League gave a ball.

JOYCE

(How dull.)

But someone is going to give a ball.

All the officers arrive in droves—and all the League members arrive in droves. Then they're shuffled together to the rhythm of a smooth band—and what happens?

(Everyone knows what happens!)

JOYCE

They all leave in pairs. They come in droves—and leave in couples. Hundreds of couples pouring out the front door, the side door, the back door even out the windows of the Fairmont Hotel! And when that happens?

(The Pay-off.)

Three debutantes are married off to three unsuspecting Naval officers, and the social season is considered a success!

MAUDE

(What an attitude to take!)

I don't know where you get your ideas—you always ridicule the social system your family has helped to build. In my day a young girl—

(Not that again!)

Now, now, Mother don't start about when you were a young girl.

(Rather have her go on about the ball.)

Just tell me about this officers' ball you cooked up this afternoon.

MAUDE

(Oh. she doesn't understand that this will be a different sort of ball.)

It isn't for the officers, Joyce. It's for all those nice sailor boys and their nice little girl friends. You can have it at the Civic Auditorium.

JOYCE

(Laughs)

(Bell bottom trousers. here we come!)

You mean for the Gobs?

MAUDE

(Really. such language.)

Gobs? I don't know what you mean by that word. I mean all those lovely boys with the little round white hats. They're all so far away from home—and so, of course, they're homesick. Oh, Joyce, it will be a wonderful thing for you girls to do something for them.

(That's it—appeal to her better self.)

JOYCE

Oh, Mother, Mother! You're so delightfully naive. Those boys wouldn't take a deb to a dance at the Civic Auditorium.

(She can't mean this.)

JOYCE

How you've changed in the last few hours—wanting me to go and with a Gob.

MAUDE

(Mercy. what an idea.)

Oh, no, darling. You girls won't go with them. They will bring their own girls. You will invite the officers, of

JOYCE

(Poor Mother. she just doesn't know.)

I can see that your social education has been sadly neglected, Mother. Have you ever watched a sailor make a date with a girl?

(And it always looks rather intriguing. too.)

She's standing there at the corner of Market and Powell—all done up in a bright red dress, with a pair of green shoes, a suede sports jacket and plenty of purple lipstick. Up comes the Gob—there's a little jockeying back and forth—and the date's on. That's the way they do it at Market and Powell.

MAUDE

(She's just trying to irritate me.)

Don't be absurd, dear. I'm serious about this.

JOYCE

(Serious? Are you?)

Well, you might just as well count me out of it—because I'm not going to have anything to do with it. Besides, I know the League won't do it.

MAUDE

(She can't cross me like this all the time.)

Of course you'll do it. Now I don't want to hear any more about it. You

130

don't have to go with one of those boys.

(Let's see—who would be nice?)

You can invite one of those nice officers you met last year.

Or Tony Craig.

JOYCE

(She's bullying me.)

I'm not going to do it, Mother. You might as well quit trying to talk me into it.

MAUDE

(This time I'm going to put my foot down.)

Of course you'll do it—

JOYCE

(Determined! Hm-m maybe this could be fun.)

All right—If I do it, you'll have to take the consequences.

MAUDE

(Now what does she mean by that?)

What kind of consequences?

JOYCE

(You can't stop me now. You asked for it!)

If I have to go through with this—
I'm going to do it my way!

(I certainly am.)

I'll go to the dance—and what's
more—I'll take me a man

(Oh this is delicious!)

And do you know where I'm going
to get him? I'm going down to Market
and Powell and pick me up a Gob!

Exercise Scene No. 4

*Seated at her telephone in her modest office is Kay
Calhoun, a young woman private investigator, who has
been retained by a church group to establish the
innocence of a man unjustly accused of a killing. Kay is
going through a list of important lawyers, trying to get
one who will handle the case of the convicted man at a
retrial. The scene opens with Kay in the middle of a
conversation with an attorney.*

KAY

*(He just doesn't want to bother with the case.
He's made up his mind.)*

If only you'll read the transcript of the trial.

(Pause.)

(He's being stubborn now. He doesn't want to reason. How can he be so unfair?)

I can't understand how you can say that before you've looked into the case.

(If he'd just see me, I know I could convince him that Mackey's innocent. I have the facts. All he'd have to do is listen.)

Well, will you let me come over and talk to you?

(Pause.)

(Stubborn piq-headed. Lawyers—Justice! He wouldn't recognize Justice if he walked right into her scales.)

That's your final answer?

(Mark him off. Mark him off.)

Well, thank you very much.

(What now? Who's left?)

(Kay hangs up the receiver, looks at her list. All the names are crossed off except one. She now crosses off that last name as she speaks into the telephone again.)

(Our last hope.)

AMHURST 915-555-1212, please.

(Pause)

(Guess lawyers are like everyone else. They believe what they want to believe.)

This is Kay Calhoun. Could I talk with Mr. Drumm?

(Pause.)

(Maybe I can drum Mackey's innocence into his head.)

Hello, Mr. Drumm, I've been retained by a church organization to investigate the Earl Mackey case.

(Of course you know about it—it's been in all the papers.)

What's that?

(Pause)

(I should give up? Don't you tell me what to do Mister! Let me tell you a thing or two.)

But Mr. Drumm, I've already started the investigation and I've certainly found enough evidence to make me doubt that he's guilty

(Pause)

(Man innocent until he's proved guilty! Humph!
Guilty until proved innocent! But how can we
Prove anything if no one will take the case?)

But it seems to me that if there is any
doubt at all, every effort should be
made to get a new trial

(Pause)

(Oh. don't be so unctuous!)

(I wish mv mother hadn't taught me to be a
lady!)

Well, thank you!

(For nothing!)

Thank you very much. Good-bye.

(And that's that. End of the list. But that's not
that—and it's not the end of the line. I'll find
someone—I'll find a lawyer Yet!)

Exercise Scene No. 5

A small room in a county building, housing courtrooms,
jail, and morgue. Ruth's mother and father have been
killed in an explosion. Ruth, accompanied by her
boyfriend, Jack, is in the building, but has just been
summoned to identify the bodies of her parents. Jack is
left alone in the room. After a considerable length of
time a detective enters.

DETECTIVE

(So this is the kid. huh. Sort of innocent-looking. His kind'll fool you. He looks nervous already.)

Sit down, Jack. You've got lots of time.

JACK

(Poor Ruth. I wish I could help her. Oh. here's the Detective. *Wonder if Ruth is still back there.)*

Where's Ruth?

DETECTIVE

(I'll play it smooth. first.)

She's tied up just now, Jack.

JACK

(She needs me with her. Poor kid.)

I want to go to her.

DETECTIVE

(You can go to he.—after You've told me what I want to know.)

After a while. Maybe she wants be alone.

JACK

(Alone! At a time like this! She needs me.)

I don't think she wants to be alone.

DETECTIVE

(So he wants to be with her. huh? Afraid she might talk. They'll talk—both of 'em.)

I think maybe she does.

(Well. I'll start with a few leading questions and get to the point.)

In the Marines, weren't you, Jack?

JACK

(Marines? What's that got to do with it?)

Yes.

DETECTIVE

(I'll get him up to the point.)

How long you in, Jack?

JACK

(What difference does it make to him?)

Little over three years.

Detective

(Hm—three years. Had time to have plenty of training with explosives.)

Ever have anything to do with depth charges?

JACK

(Depth charges? Me? I was a wireless operator. What's going on here?)

No. I was a wireless operator.

DETECTIVE

(Wireless operator. He'd know how to rig up a time bomb. I'll lead him a little more.)

Know how to fix a radio, I suppose?

JACK

(This guy is trying to find out something. What's he driving at?)

Why—sure.

DETECTIVE

(I'll bet you do.)

Fixed any lateley?

(Fixed any lately? This guy's nuts. What's really on his mind? What would I be doing fixing radios?)

Why—no.

DETECTIVE

(He'll try to alibi out of this.)

Thought maybe you had found some wire in the glove compartment of your car.

JACK

(What's he doing in the glove compartment of my car?)

Wire?

DETECTIVE

(Want to play dumb. huh? Might as well start putting the

Where did you get that wire, Jack?

JACK

(There's not any wire in my car. What's he asking me all these questions for?)

I don't know what you're talking about.

DETECTIVE

(He knows what I'm talking about.)

Oh, yes you do, Jack. That was part of the wire you used on the dynamite.

JACK

(Dynamite. does he think I had something to do with—oh. mv God!)

What are you talking about?

DETECTIVE

(Now. I've got him! He's excited ok—I'll let him squirm a little.)

The dynamite you took out to the yacht.

JACK

(He's—God! I Can't believe-)

Dynamite to the yacht?

DETECTIVE

(He's squirming a lot now!)

The dynamite you took out to the yacht and wired up to the alarm clock.

JACK

(This guy's trying to make trouble for me—I've got to get out—aet away—I haven't done any-thing.)

Wired to an alarm clock!

DETECTIVE

(Now—he breaking. He was in on it. all right.)

Where did you get the dynamite, Jack?

JACK

(This man thinks I had something to do with the murder. How could he think such a thing. I never had anything to do with dynamite in my life. I don't like where this is going!)

I never saw any dynamite.

DETECTIVE

Yea, I know—but where did you get it? Probably stole it somewhere—say!

JACK

(He's crazy—I'm being framed—I'm scared—)

No—I...

DETECTIVE

(He's fumbling for an answer now. He stole it from the Marine Corps. sure as hell.)

You bought it?

JACK

(I'm scared—I don't know what to do-)

No—I...

DETECTIVE

You sure had a motive.)

Ruth's a wealthy girl now!

(You knew about this money. boy.)

You know that, don't you, Jack?

JACK

(Money—What's that got to do with me?)

How would I know...

DETECTIVE

(They both had a motive. Looks like they were both in on it. He didn't have the money to swing it. but Ruth did!)

Did Ruth buy the dynamite?

JACK

(You lousy. You son-of-...! He's accusing)

What's she got to do with this?

DETECTIVE

(Yep! She gave him the money and he bought the dynamite.)

Or—did you buy it yourself?

JACK

(What's he talking about—?)

Did I buy what myself. I don't know what you're talking about.

(This is bad.)

I want to get out of here.

DETECTIVE

(It'll be a long time before you get out of her. kid. You might as well open up.)

Well—you might be here quite a while yet.

(All right. smart guy. I've had enough of this. Let's let him have it!)

Come on kid. Why did you murder them?

(Let's see how you take that?)

JACK

*(Me—murder? Oh. God! Why I never even—
where's Ruth. What are they doing to Ruth?
We're being accused of-)*

Murder?

At first you will probably think and react as
you believe you are supposed to. That won't ring
true and the audience will know it.

You must dual-track in the *character's image.* Of
course, what the character means to you—what
you are able to make out of it, will always reflect a
little of *your own personal* self. A certain amount of
you, the *actor's own ego,* is necessary to every characterization. This creates energy and impact.

CHAPTER EIGHTEEN

The Diaphragm
(How To Control It)

You have been breathing all your life but chances are you haven't been breathing correctly for a long time. With your good posture, stand in front of a mirror. Put one hand on your chest and the other on the upper part of your abdomen.

Take a big deep breath.

Did your chest swell up? Did you get small around the waist? If so, you need some reminders about correct natural breathing.

We have in the lower part of the thorax, or chest cavity, a floor of muscle that is also the roof of the abdominal cavity, separating one from the other. This is the diaphragm.

Try an experiment by lying down on the floor. Just relax. Don't even think about your breathing. Place your hands flat against your floating ribs at the sides and notice how the entire region, all the way around to the back contracts and expands as you breathe, while your chest remains immobile. Notice too, how the floating ribs now seem to have a very direct contact with the diaphragm.

Stand up and attach your chest, fixed and high, to your imaginary hook. Breathe just as you did while you were lying on the floor again.

It may seem strange for you to breathe this way, especially if you've always been told to take deep breaths with your chest (another "old wives' tale"). But don't be disturbed about it, you are now following nature's way of breathing, and she'll also help you acquire the habit of breathing in her own sensible manner. Nature is on your side.

All animals breathe in this fashion. You breathed in the same correct, natural way when you were an infant.

Here is a coordinating exercise in breathing and performing a specific action at the same time.

Start from a sitting position with hands on knees. As you inhale, move one hand up to your top shirt button. Start the movement and a breath at the same instant. End the movement at the top shirt button at the exact peak of your intake of breath.

As you exhale, return the hand to its original position (on the knee) arrive at this original position at the same instant, as the final expiration of your breath takes place.

By coordinating a movement exactly with your breathing, you have experienced again, the use of a power tool of acting. So keep practicing until you have it cold.

Focus your mind on diaphragmatic breathing and let your mind tell your body what to do. You will soon get back to breathing as well as you did when you were born.

Nature intended that you should breathe with the diaphragm. It's healthful for your general well being in daily living, and it's necessary to you as an actor. With diaphragmatic breathing, you control the breath and get compressed air, necessary for keeping balanced energy under all the vibrations of the speech instrument.

As you may know, compressed air is one of the strongest forces of power known in the world. It's used to stop trains, to drive pneumatic drills and in many other mechanical processes requiring enormous power.

To acquire vocal vitality and control, make use of the same kind of power that science has found so useful. Nature has already given you the necessary equipment.

Later we will go more extensively into the use of this source of power in speech. Meanwhile, breathe easily, rhythmically, and diaphragmatically.

The following poem can be used as a muscular exercise to strengthen the muscles that control the diaphragm. Whisper the poem in a bass-baritone whisper using no sound—with a high fixed chest (no movement of the chest.)

The whispering exercise will help develop the habit of breathing from the diaphragm. It also develops control of the air as it leaves the lungs. Control of the breathing out process is more important than control of the breathing in process.

You may become dizzy when you first try this exercise, and you will feel your diaphragm is pulling up inside the lung cage. That's good! Just make sure that you don't stop the rich outflow of air by tightening your throat.

Exercise—Big Black Broncs*
(No movement of upper chest!)

Big black broncs in a round wooden pen,
Round pen cowboys; with ropes and spurs,
Slapped and cracked and pounded on the hide,
Pounded on the hide.
Beat that timer with all my might
Hard as I was able
Fight, Fight, Fight
With flying hoofs, a buck and a boom.
Boomlay, Boomlay, Boomlay, Boom!
Then I had religion, then I had a vision
I could not turn from his revel in derision.
Then I saw the bronco walking through the dust,
Lower his head in love and trust..

(* From *Collected Poems by Lee Pennington*)

148

Starting now and in your daily practice of the poem, whisper the entire poem twice. Hold one hand on your chest, the other against your floating ribs. Keep your chest absolutely immobile, no matter how difficult it may be at first.

Whispering strengthens the muscles in the region of the diaphragm and places the power of these muscles squarely behind the column of breath. It also allows the small delicate muscles of the throat to relax and builds up general muscle tone throughout the entire body system.

Every time you get a part, get someplace by yourself and rehearse the entire role in a loud whisper before doing anything else. This will solve many problems and improve your voice at the same time.

Dustin Hoffman could tell you that whispering will work wonders for you and that's no secret!

CHAPTER NINETEEN

The Voice
(And How To Use It!)

Over the past weeks you have flexed your mental muscles and had a good physical work-out. You've explored the resources of the mind for tools of acting. You are able to make your body serve you expressively. You can apply the mechanics of timing through proper use of the mind and body.

You have accomplished a lot, but as yet we've done nothing about your voice. And acting is composed of three basic elements. The body, the mind, *and the voice*! It's time to take up voice and diction.

Most people are born with an *instrument* that can be used to produce a good voice. But only a few learn to use that instrument *correctly*. Wrong use builds up a system of tensions that keep the voice instrument from functioning properly to the best advantage.

Voice is sound produced by air passing through the larynx and made audible by vibrations of the vocal cords. You may have heard that your voice is produced in the mask of your face, in some spot in the sinus region or in the throat. *None of that is true!* The only place you can produce a vocal sound or make a vocal noise is in the Adam's apple.

That projection called the Adam's apple is formed by thyroid cartilage, and is part of the larynx. Inside the Adam's apple are two small bands of membrane, *the vocal cords*. They come together with a slightly downward motion and vibrate by means of compressed air to produce the sound called voice.

When you have had a sore throat, have you ever had a sore Adam's apple? Of course not! If you have ever suffered from laryngitis, you will remember that your throat was not noticeably sore. You just couldn't talk.

The sound produced by the vibrations of the vocal cord down in the Adam's apple is not very big. But, that sound is enlarged and enriched by overtones produced by a series of "echoes" in the various nasal, oral and chest chambers.

There is no actual sound originating in the sinus cavities, the nasal cavities, the mouth, or the chest. There are only *sympathetic air and sound vibrations*, which are set into motion by the vibrations of the vocal cords.

The combinations of sympathetic air and sound vibrations disturbs the air like ripples in a pool when a pebble is thrown into the water. The disturbed air, which we call sound waves, passes out into the atmosphere. It is picked up by the "receiving set," in our ears, or other ears, living or mechanical and is reconverted into sound as we hear it.

If you put too much uncontrolled power behind your voice, the "ripples" will be distorted, destroying the rhythmic sound patterns, just as heaving a big rock into a pool would cause distorted ripples that pile up and overlap each other. Control of possible distortion is becoming more and more important as microphones, laser discs, and even tape, and so forth are improved all the time.

Through exercises you can develop the affinity of your echo chambers (nasal, oral and chest) for the sympathetic air and sound vibrations, set into motion by the vibrating vocal cords.

The mouth and the throat act as resonating chambers and have sympathetic air and sound vibrations all their own. They also act like the bell of a trumpet or megaphone to project these combined vibrations into space. A variety of sounds can be made by vibrating the vocal cords. The sounds or noises, blended together and chopped-up by mechanical movements of the lips and tongue, become speech.

The simple vocal sounds made by the vocal cords are known as vowels.

The mechanical actions made up by the lips and tongue are called consonants.

Some consonants are silent; others have vibrations. These are called voiceless and voiced sonants and surds. In English, when a voiceless consonant ends a syllable, it should be followed by a slight puff of air.

Voiced consonants should have the same vibrations, whether used at the beginning or end of a syllable.

"A tight throat" stifles the vowel sounds and causes the consonants to be tense and strained or to be left out all together. It also distorts the rhythmic sound patterns.

Sit in front of a mirror. Lift your tongue and look at the under side of it. You can see that it's a mass of muscle. Tighten the muscle as tight as you can, and you will find that your throat will become tight and rigid, too. Feel your throat with your fingers; notice how tense it is.

Next, relax the muscles under the tongue. Focus your conscious your tongue and keep it relaxed. Letting the *tongue remain relaxed*, try to tighten any part of your throat. Impossible! It can't be done.

You have reduced the entire business of keeping a relaxed throat, to this simple training of the tongue.

The tongue has two sets of muscles, extrinsic and intrinsic. The set of muscles you use to both tighten and relax your throat are the *extrinsic* muscles. They are used primarily for swallowing.

Through tensions and inhibitions, which bring about bad habits, a great many people use their set of extrinsic muscles for speaking as well as for swallowing. The results are bad speech in general and sluggish unclear consonants.

The *intrinsic* muscles are those which lengthen and shorten the tongue, flatten and thicken it. They are the muscles you use when you cleanly and clearly make the mechanical actions called consonants.

With a little concentration and well-directed application of effort, it's easy to train the extrinsic and intrinsic muscles to perform *independently*.

Now, we need to find out how, and in what way to make the vocal cords vibrate. Somewhere in your anatomy you must produce the *power* to bring about the vibrations.

Your mental commands to produce a sound you can hear causes the vocal cords to click down together, closing the open passage in the larynx. The vocal cords act like two, taut rubber bands, placed side by side parallel. The breath current vibrates these two edges.

You probably created a similar effect as a youngster, when you put two blades of grass into your mouth and blew, causing the blades to vibrate simultaneously.

You must also know that the little sound produced by the breath current vibrating the vocal cords is *enlarged* by means of *sympathetic air* and sound vibrations set up in the echo chambers of the head and chest. These head and chest echo chambers are cavities of different sizes. Echoes from the various sized chambers differ in tone according to the length of the vibrations, just as the tone of a piano note depends in part on the length of its string. The *longer* the string the *slower* the *vibrations* and the fuller and deeper in tone. Refer to our exercise poem, "Big Black Broncs." Keep the chest high; without any movement of the chest, keep the *tongue relaxed* thus leaving the throat open. Whisper each line twice, then aloud twice— *without changing the whispering position of the throat.* (This is important!)

Be very careful not to change anything you've learned—keep the tongue relaxed. At this point, there isn't any need to worry about diction.

If your throat becomes tired, it's because you have tightened the extrinsic muscles of the tongue. Let those muscles remain relaxed and be sure that your chest does not *move*.

If you feel your throat tightening, put a pencil or cork in between your front teeth (as you do this exercise). This makes it impossible for your tongue to move much, thus keeping your throat relaxed.

After you have practiced this exercise you will notice the quality of your speaking voice change a great deal. The lower frequencies begin to come into it. The voice becomes much richer and has a more solid texture. The quality, just like the "quality of mercy"—is no longer "strained."

CHAPTER TWENTY

Speaking English Correctly
(And Incorrectly, Correctly)

Scientific improvements in the acoustics of the legitimate theater and the electronic developments in sound systems in motion picture theaters and television sets have made it possible for audiences to hear the performer more clearly than ever before.

In theaters or at home on television, actors' speech can now be directed intimately to each one in an audience.

Each individual in the audience likes to understand what he's hearing and make up his own mind as to the truth and realism.

The actor's job is greater because he no longer performs for an audience as a group. He is now performing for a group of individual thinkers. Each of these individuals bases his critical judgement, either consciously or subconsciously (audible or not) on remembering experiences of his own or someone else's.

Words, their use, sound, meaning, and cleanness of delivery are tools of the actor. The actor's responsibility is to execute these words *cleanly* and *clearly*: to *sound* pleasing and natural and above all to do it with such ease and dexterity that it will produce excitement.

Words—like everything else—are made up of something: We need to break them down, to better understand them. They have two parts, *sound* and *action*. They also have a beginning and an end. Each sound and each action, each beginning and each end are of equal importance.

The separate parts of each word must be executed with such expert balanced vitality, volume, and control that the audience will be able to understand without conscious effort. Each individual's sound system (ear) should receive sound vibrations that translate exactly and clearly, without any distortion. This is where *balanced vitality* comes into play. (Not to be confused with accent or stress.) The area we're getting into now is of utmost importance!

With a few exceptions, the parts of words can for all practical purposes be reduced to *ten sounds* and *five actions*.

Ten Sounds with Diacritical Marks

		Key Words
1. ä	as in	father
2. ō	as in	so
3. o͞o	as in	soon
4. e	as in	see
5. ĭ	as in	hit
6. ĕ	as in	deck
7. a	as in	had
8 o͝o	as in	hook
9. ŭ	as in	luck
10. ạ	as in	law

The Actions Are:

Action	Explanation	Letter Produced
1. Lips together, then opened.	Three slightly different thoughts and pressures.	b p m
2. Tongue strikes against gum line of upper front teeth— then relaxes	Four slightly different thoughts and pressures	l d t n

3. Back tongue meets	Two slightly different	g
soft palate, then	different thoughts	k
relaxes	and pressures.	
4. Lower lip against	Two slightly different	v
upper front teeth	thoughts and pressures.	f
5. Blade of tongue and	A buzz and a hiss	z
hard ridge back of		s
upper teeth		

Final r's are pronounced like the "er" in the word ermine.

The "-ing" sound must be executed with the nostrils open, not closed.

"Wh" is pronounced h$\overline{oo}$.

Two of the actions can be combined to produce what is known as double-consonant combinations. The most common double consonant combinations in the English language are: bl, br, cl, cr, dr, fl, fr, gl, gr, pl, pr, sh, zh, sm, sl, sn, sp, sq, st, sw, ch, sc, tr plus two executions of the consonant combinations, th: (this and thick).

There are a few consonantal diphthongs: They are the soft g, j, and x.

One conso-vowel: The beginning r and one conso-vowel combination: qu.

In English there are very few triple consonant combinations. Some of the m$\overline{os}$t common are: chr, spr, sch, scl, scr, spl, and shr.

W is always pronounced $\overline{oo}$

Y is always pronounced e

In ordinary American speech: "The" before a word beginning with a consonant is *always* pronounced thŭ (except for emphasis). "The" before a word beginning with a vowel is al*ways* pronounced thē. "A" before a word beginning with a consonant is always pronounced ŭ (except for emphasis). "A" before a vowel is an.

By combining two of the ten sounds, we can produce the six "sound combinations," or diphthongs, that are most frequently used.

The first sound in a diphthong is called a "prime," because it is the stronger of the two. The second sound is called the "vanish." It is the weaker of the two. Here are the diphthongs in the American English language:

Prime		*Vanish*		*Diphthong*		*Key Word*
ĕ	plus	ē	equals	ā	as in	hate
ä	plus	ē	equals	ī	as in	might
ō	plus	ōō	equals	ō	as in	hope
ē	plus	ōō	equals	ū	as in	cute
ä	plus	ōō	equals	ou	as in	house
a̤	plus	ē	equals	oi	as in	boil

All words are made up of single, double, or triple actions (consonants) and single sounds (vowels) or combined sounds (diphthongs).

If you will think of consonants as being actions, you're more likely to execute them completely. They should be *fully executed* whether they come at the beginning, in the middle, or at the end of a word.

The same rule applies for a sound, regardless of if it's a single sound or a combination of sounds, they should be fully executed.

The professional actor must be flexib*le* and *adaptable*.

Sometimes the actor must correctly speak incorrect diction. This merely requires substituting sounds or actions that are common to the local speech or dialect as they are needed for the characterization.

When the actor turns his attention seriously to sound, he finds he has many new concepts and tools to use.

Thousands of man-hours and dollars have been spent to reproduce perfectly the voice vibrations made by the human instrument. Comparatively few man-hours and dollars have been spent by the actor exploring the possibilities and the further development of the human vibrator. The audience has spent many more hours training their ears and developing emotional expectancy than the actor has in fulfilling the audience's expectations.

The actor must be *understandable the first time through*! The audience can't go back and run over a difficult passage, as the audience of a book, magazine, or newspaper can. The *eye receives more quickly* and *retains longer than the ear*. The ear is as easily tired by a monotonous sound or speech pattern, as by uninteresting dialogue.

Diction is not as difficult as it seems; it is just confusing because in English we have two languages. The *written* and the *spoken*. Don't worry about it too much, just pronounce all the sounds and execute all the actions, then you will be all right. After all, as an actor you have to talk. But more importantly, *you must be understood*!

God has given you everything you need to speak correctly, if you will but use the gift correctly and naturally.

In the past I have worked with many actors who have developed bad habits and incorrect methods before coming to me. Mostly, because of poor training they were taught in such a way they had become "affected" and unnatural. I would always rather work with people who either have had no training at all, or actors who have been taught to be natural and "unaffected" in all their acting.

I realize it's not easy for you to always *"come across"* as *natural*, but as you train it gets easier, believe me!

CHAPTER TWENTY-ONE

Interpretation
(With Emphasis And Connotation)

Did you ever have a friend ask, "What was that again?" as you finished telling them something?

Then after repeating exactly what you had said—this time stressing certain *key* words for *emphasis*, and giving them a special *connotation* to bring out a particular significance beyond their literal and obvious meaning—your friend nodded his head showing he finally understood you.

Audiences can't ask, "What was that again?"

Actors need to use stress and connotation as tools of interpretation. These tools can answer every possible question that the line prompts in the mind of the listener.

Every sentence has several words in it which might give the answer to specific questions.

For instance, take the line, "This is Carol Burnett speaking to you." There are at least seven questions you could answer in this single remark. Read the line accenting or stressing the first word, "This."

"This is Carol Burnett speaking to you." You have not only established, but emphasized, the identity of the speaker.

Accent the word "Carol" and you know which member of the Burnett family is speaking. If you accent the word "Burnett," you stress which particular Carol is speaking. Not Carol Jones or Carol Smith, but Carol Burnett. Stress the word "speaking" and that answers the question of what Carol Burnett is doing.

Accent the word "to" and it's clear that she is talking.

By accenting the word "you," there is little doubt to whom Carol Burnett is talking.

The variety of meanings you can acquire by the ability to stress and give special connotation to any word in a line gives the line *authority, energy,* and *color!*

In the first line of the "Quality of Mercy" speech, Portia says, "The quality of mercy is not strain'd."

Carol Burnett would be able to answer all the parenthetical questions in that single phrase:

(The What?)...The quality...(of what?)...of mercy (is not what?)...is not strain'd.

By answering these three questions in the

phrase its reading gains much more color and vividness than it would have if the actor thought of it as answering only one question.

Practice the "Quality of Mercy" speech answering each of the following parenthetical questions.

Exercise

The quality (of what?) of mercy (is not what?) is not strain'd, (it what?) It droppeth (as what?) as the gentle rain (from where?) from heaven, (to where?) upon the place beneath: (It is what?) it is twice bless'd; It blesseth (whom?) him that gives and him that takes: (How great is it?) 'Tis mightiest in the mightiest; (How does it affect kings?) It becomes the throned monarch, (How?) better than his crown; (Why?) His scepter shows the force (of what?) of temporal power, (What's that?) The attribute to awe and majesty, Wherein doth sit (the what?) the dread and fear of kings; But, (But what?) mercy is above, (Above what?) this scepter'd sway, (Why?) It is enthroned in the hearts of kings. It is an attribute (to whom?) to God himself, and earthly power doth then show likest God's. (When does mercy become thus?) When mercy seasons justice. the five W's and an H that will help you with stress and connotation. Who, what, when where, why, and how.

Using the "Quality of Mercy" speech, controlled by the five W's and an H as a pattern, read aloud as much as possible. Especially read dialogue. This will give you a solid interpretative background, and prepare you to take the fast direction, that is so necessary in today's fast paced production of motion pictures and television.

If you will consciously practice answering these "who, what, when, where, why, and how" questions, you will develop *word flexibility* and be able to get more out of the scenes in an earlier Chapter 16.

This may seem like a fairly simple process, and it really is, but what dividends it pays. You can make this a three way exercise by whispering it, the first couple of times through.

CHAPTER TWENTY-TWO

Market Your Craft
(Selling—The New You)

"First impressions are lasting impressions." That is so true in the motion picture business.

In this business, the first impressions can sometimes be the last impression.

Producers, directors, and casting people are busy and talented people. The deciding factor in giving an unknown (or even an experienced actor whose opportunities have been limited) a chance to read for a part is often based on first impressions.

It's up to you to know how to handle yourself during an interview: how to be at ease, and how to be well-poised. How to sell yourself; and how not to oversell yourself.

Sandy Dennis, who rose from television commercials in Los Angeles to star in her own television series, worked for weeks to make the right impression when she got her first important interview.

At the appointed time, she stepped buoyantly into the office—tripped and fell flat on her beautiful face.

Sandy's world went black, but only for a moment, for months of training came to the rescue. She showed such poise and quick judgment in neither making too much nor too little of the incident that the director had her read immediately for the part. When she left his office the role was hers. The accidental fall itself turned out to be unimportant. What counted was his first impression of her *professional poise.*

To be as unshakably poised, as this young actress, is much more a matter of sound technique than of serene temperament.

Don't be fooled by the casual manner of a casting director. You may be sure he's studying you: looking you over like a piece of merchandise. He's no window shopper either. When he looks, it's because he wants to buy!

Always have professional pictures of yourself and be ready to show them without apologies or explanations. Your graduation picture won't do, nor will gimmicky "outer space" types of pictures. The pictures should show *YOU.* Some head shots, showing a fair range of moods; others, in various types of wardrobe.

Have extra prints of each picture. Your interviewer may want to keep one or two. Make certain that your name, address and phone number are on the back (or that of your agent's). It's much better to have your resume stapled on the back of the picture with all the vital information (preferably typed neatly). Don't be misled into thinking that the pictures he rejects are "no good." Almost every interviewer is likely to make a different selection. Each has his own professional purpose and his own taste as valid reasons for his choice. For the sake of efficiency and economy it's a good idea to have several 8 x 10 composites made up with more than one pose (usually four) on each one.

On your neatly typed outline, stapled to the back of your pictures, be honest. Don't invent non-existent credits that won't bear checking out. You can't afford to have your name mixed up in this type of deception. You'll only identify yourself as an impostor, or to use a "show business term," "a phony."

If your only appearance anywhere has been as a member of the church choir back home, fine, say so. Everyone has to start somewhere.

Deborah Kerr began her career as the curtain raiser for a show in Bristol, England. No one outside Bristol and probably very few Bristolites— particularly noticed this modest debut of an actress who had studied long and faithfully to prepare herself for intercontinental stardom. Nevertheless it was a beginning—a good one.

It will look better and be far more plausible if you will state in your outline that you've put your time and effort studying with a well-known teacher rather than making up a list of phony credits.

Perhaps your teacher will give you a card stating your credentials. Some teachers and coaches periodically give the unestablished actor a card stating how long he has studied and what in his opinion he is capable of doing at that time. These cards help the actor in getting interviews and protect the drama coach, from the overeager job seekers, who claim to be a client of theirs after only one lesson.

Some of the first questions you'll be asked are:

"Tell me about yourself."

"What have you done?"

"Is there any film on you?"

You are in a spot now; however, every beginning actor has been in that exact same spot. Just remember every *actor* had to be a "beginning actor" at one time.

Always tell the truth. If you have no film, say so. If you have no professional stage credits, say so.

However, there is a way out. Almost every casting director will help you. Ask for a chance to read for him, or to audition a scene that you have already prepared. He's looking for talent, and he will usually give you a scene if you don't have one.

You can take it home, study it, then go back and do it for him. If he likes the way you do it, he will indicate your next move.

After you have begun to establish yourself as a working actor, you may get jobs on a "cold reading"—that means reading a part on sight with no preparation. This takes real talent and mechanics. Remember not to read too fast and to listen to the other person reading with you.

Rehearsed or cold, your reading will give you something extremely important: exposure and *where it counts*. My students spend an additional eight weeks on interviewing and cold reading alone! We think it's that important.

He may not need you today, however, he will remember you tomorrow. He will remember how you read, how you handled yourself, and whether you were able to live up to your claims.

He casts something every day, month in and month out, year after year. He knows better than anyone else that there is a definite place for the *well-trained* beginner. Almost everyone connected with casting is willing to give promising new people a hearing.

I want to interject this important point. In New York, Hollywood and other large cities where there are "agents" and "casting directors," there will always be a "fringe edge," where the so-called operators have only one thing in mind from the second you walk into their office. That one thing is to separate you from your money! They want to sell you pictures and give you acting lessons *before* they can represent you or "cast you in something." This type of "scam" has nothing to do with the *real* business and it's a *blot* on our industry, but it does exist. A business totally devoted to making a living off of actors' and actresses' hopes and dreams, by inferring that they can help you "make it," but of course you'll have to pay them for pictures and so forth, is not a legitimate business. A good rule is, if they ask for money, *in any way*, turn around and walk out of their office and don't ever go back! It's a shame that this has to exist, but all large industries across the nation have these "scam artists" who seem to exist somehow.

At the present time, all professionals must belong to at least one of the organizations in the "Four A's." The "Four A's" stand for the Associated Actors and Artists of America. (There are more than four now, but they are still called the Four A's.)

Among them are AFTRA (American Federation of Television & Radio Artists), SAG (Screen Actors Guild), Equity (Actors Equity Association), AGMA (American Guild of Musical Artists), AGVA (American Guild of Variety Artists), and SEG (Screen Extras Guild), which is devoted primarily to the interests of people appearing as general atmosphere in motion pictures and in filmed television.

Under the Taft-Hartley Law, a newcomer is allowed 30 days after his first professional

172

performance before he is obliged to join one of the professional guilds or unions. The one he joins first becomes his parent union. There is a reciprocal agreement among the Four A's that acts in favor of the performer who works in the various mediums under their jurisdiction.

Getting back to auditioning, when an interview is over leave—don't drag it out—wasting the interviewer's time and your own as well. If you've left pictures or a list of credits with the interviewer, tell the secretary on your way out of the office. Give her an extra word of thanks when you say good-bye.

Secretaries fill a highly specialized position in the business. Often, they are the trusted "antennae" of their bosses. Besides as guardians of the "portals thru which you seek to pass," they can sometimes open the door to courteous and appreciative actors. The old adage applies here better than ever, "the harder you work, the luckier you get."

With your knowledge and use of the tools of acting, it won't take these serious buyers of talent very long to use you. You will make these casting people "look good" and they know it.

I must tell you not to "change horses in the middle of the stream." Many careers have been lost just this way. Remember, what frustration is to yesterday, apprehension is to tomorrow. These two clever characters will always try to inch their way into your mind, especially when you don't have the ability or confidence quite yet.

When patience and forbearance persist, these two thieves don't have a chance as *persistence* is more important than ability, skill, talent, or anything else. If you keep trying with determination, you *will* "get there." Especially when determination has been commissioned by a long tradition of faithful and loyal actors that have gone on before you, true to their calling to the end.

You need to have the ability to accept disappointment by not expecting everything at first. You'll learn to laugh in the face of setbacks and respond with a pleasant understanding spirit when you can "cool it" while others around you curse it. Just say to your self, "I refuse to be hassled by delays and conflicting facts because I know who is in control and it will happen at the right time, just as everything that happens to me is for my highest and best use (Rom. 8:28).

If you'll say to yourself, I'm going to stay calm and cheerful, relaxed and refreshed. Know what? You really will! Without pills, booze, astrology charts, or "hocus pocus." I can't promise you that others will always understand.

You see we have another problem right now. Do you remember back in the second chapter when I told you about walking through that threshold, on your own? It's time.

CHAPTER TWENTY-THREE

Freedom From Bondage
(The Truth Shall Set You Free—John 8:32)

As an American educator, Horace Mann once described what makes us the way we are: "We are all creatures of habit. Habit is a cable; we weave a thread of it every day, and at last we cannot break it." So we can either be slaves to our habits or develop habits that serve us.

This is precisely what we have done and now you have the necessary tools (habits) to attain your highest desires. All of your most noble dreams may now be realized. The only thing between you and your goal is application of the knowledge you now possess.

My ninety-eight-year-old grandmother has always reminded me, "Be careful what you go after, you just might get it."

I had a hard time understanding for many years what she meant, but I now know she was really trying to tell me not to lower my standards and to keep a "good sense of values."

I remember two things vividly from my high school chemistry class. First, I removed a wart from the back of my right thumb through applications of sulfuric acid for thirty-three consecutive days. Second, I watched the slow death of a frog in an unforgettable experiment.

My teacher put the poor frog in a large glass jar of cool water. Beneath the jar, he put a Bunsen burner with a small flame. The temperature rose ever so gradually that the frog was never aware of the change. Three hours later, the frog was dead...boiled to death! The change occurred so slowly that the frog neither tried to jump out nor let out a kick.

Attentive as I was to the gruesome exhibition I didn't realize I was witnessing a profound principle that would remind me of that frog for the rest of my life.

> The thorns which I have reaped are of the tree
> I planted; they have torn me, and I bleed.
> I should have known what fruit
> Would spring from such a seed.
>
> —Byron

You will remember David's son, Solomon. He had it all, wisdom, wealth, fame, and unparalleled achievement.

Things began to change so slowly, however, that even he didn't see it coming. Almost as if he had attained the mastery of man and God, he seized the reins of *compromise and wrong* and drove himself to the cloudy flats of licentiousness, pride, lust, and idolatry. Just as insane Nero in later history, Solomon became irrational, sensual and even skeptical of things he once held precious.

Layers of dust collected in the majestic temple he had built now that the king had turned his attention to another project. The building of strange edifices for the strange gods he and his strange wives were now serving. Solomon (like many other absolute monarchs, top business executives, athletic prima donas, or some film stars I've known) simply drove too fast and traveled too far.

Solomon died a debauched, effeminate, cynic, so satiated with materialism that life was all "vanity and striving after wind" (Ecclesiastes 2:26). He left a nation confused, in conflict, and soon to be fractured by civil war.

What has all this to do with your acting career? Let me assure you it has everything to do with it!

An actor should be a fine individual with high moral standards, ethics, and scruples that can stand up to the magnifying glass tactics of the most unscrupulous "gossip rags" and "rumor magazines."

And this is the ideal that most professionals start out with, but as we have seen, habits and standards never "suddenly" change or crumble. No marriage "suddenly" breaks down. No nation "suddenly" become a mediocre power, and no person "suddenly" becomes a slave to his own habits overnight.

Slowly, almost imperceptibly, certain things are accepted that were once rejected. Things once considered hurtful are now secretly tolerated. At the outset it appears harmless, perhaps even exciting, but the wedge it brings leaves a gap that grows wider as moral decline joins hands with spiritual decay. The gap widens into a canyon. As Solomon said, "That way which seems right becomes the way of death." He ought to know.

So be extremely careful about lowering your standards and allowing harmful habits that correspond with your desires, to shackle you, for what this book is really about is "A good sense of values!" For without a good set of values you can master all the material presented here and still never have an inch of film shot on you.

Be cautious about becoming inflated with your own importance. Be alert to the pitfalls of prosperity and success. Should God grant riches and fame, don't run scared or feel guilty. Just stay *balanced*. Remember Solomon, who went from a humble man of wisdom to a vain fool, in a short span of time.

I'm now grateful for that chemistry class back in 1955, in Dodge City, Kansas. At the time I thought, "What a drag." Not any more. The memory of that frog has kept me out of a lot of hot water.

You may ask yourself, "What's the secret, the formula to attain my goals? How can I win and be used for *my* highest and best purposes?"

It's really very simple. So simple you won't believe it. All it takes is one word, perhaps the easiest word in the English language to say. Properly used that single syllable carries more weight than tons of good intentions, and I'll tell you that word in just a moment. But, first I want to remind you to give any potential bad habits a "firm shove" away from your life, the moment you identify them. (You'll always know them by their fruit, and they will *always* try to take a piece of your freedom.) *Your freedom from bondage* is so much greater than any temporary excitement or pleasure.

As you know, we are all a product of our own thoughts. Thoughts form the thermostat which regulates what we accomplish in life. My body responds and reacts to the input of my mind. It must; it's another natural law. If I feed my mind with doubt or worry, that is precisely what I will experience. If I adjust my thermostat forward—to thoughts filled with vision, hope, and ultimate victory, I can expect to win! *You and I become what we think about.*

If anything, or anyone causes you *mental physical*, or *emotional bondage*, get rid of it, or them. You can do this by asking yourself what the *real truth* is. The Bible says in John 8:32, "You will know the truth, and the truth shall set you free."

Keep your enthusiasm and incentive going and growing stronger every day. A vision of a goal of where you want to go is just as important as a realistic view of where you are now.

Wherefore I perceive that there is nothing better than that a man should rejoice in his own works; for that is his portion.

—*Ecclesiastes 3:22*

I must warn you of one more slick little guy that can stop you and your acting career cold! He can pick any lock and get in anywhere unsuspecting minds are taking their rest. (I always think of him as a spring-loaded button that I can mentally keep pressed down in my mind, for if I let go, he is loose to hurt me.)

His name—Procrastination. He will strip you without a blink of remorse. He will always be standing there no matter how many times you defeat him.

So watch out for him! The procrastinator doesn't mean to be that way, but the robber is so clever at rearranging the facts just enough to gain your sympathies.

Even when others call his character into question, you could find yourself not only believing in him, but actually quoting and defending him.

Too late you'll see through his disguises and give him grudgingly credit as the shrewdest thief of all.

Some never come to such a realization at all! They stroll down to their graves arm-in-arm with the very robber who has stolen away their lives.

Procrastination! His specialty is stealing your enthusiasm and dedication. He will always strike when you're at your weakest.

You step on the scales to weigh yourself and stare in disbelief. The scales tell you the truth—but the thief offers another interpretation. Stealing your surge and motivation, he whispers the major word *tomorrow*. You reach for something else to eat just to confirm it.

You have a crucial decision! It's been building up for quite a while now. You may have even ignored it or postponed it before. But now you must not do so again nor wait another hour.

Today is "D Day!"

Now, back to that one little word I promised. I'll make you a deal. I'll tell you the word only if you'll promise to use it the next time you're tempted to give in to that fast-talking time and energy embezzler called procrastination.

I have a warning, however; it may be easy to say—but it will require all the discipline and faith you have.

The word is "NOW."